Oxford *Smart*

QUEST 1

ENGLISH LANGUAGE AND LITERATURE

TEACHER BOOK

Helen Backhouse
Jane Branson
Jenny Roberts

OXFORD
UNIVERSITY PRESS

Contents

Chapter 2

Chapter 3

Welcome to Quest

Quest delivers the 11–14 segment of the *Oxford Smart* Curriculum Service for English and has been written to:

- build on the variety of learner experiences at KS2 and explore English as a unique discipline, empowering, engaging and motivating both learners and teachers
- support teachers in delivering a diverse, relevant and challenging curriculum, drawing on the varied and disparate identities and interests of KS3 students and validating their experiences and ideas
- look back across the rich literary heritage of English Literature but also forwards to a future dominated by the digital world
- provide access to high-quality texts from a wide range of writers, both classic and contemporary, and from a range of backgrounds, cultures and experiences
- offer flexibility and choice while still delivering the core skills and knowledge so that teachers can customise their route through the resources and choose from alternative source texts to best suit the needs of their students
- enable efficient and effective progress tracking, giving teachers the confidence that students will be ready to embark on their GCSE studies by the end of Year 9
- allow teachers to identify and address misconceptions and misunderstandings with low-stakes assessments plus intervention before moving on.

The *Oxford Smart* Curriculum Service

The *Oxford Smart* Curriculum Service for English is aligned to and develops the skills and knowledge essential for accessing the KS3 and KS4 National Curriculum for English. It is underpinned by six core curriculum pillars which connect content, pedagogy, assessment and data to deliver a coherent and responsive learning experience. The curriculum has been built on a strong foundation of pedagogical research and will generate its own evidence and impact from experts, educators and learners. Over time, this portfolio of evidence will inform and inspire future curriculum evaluation and development, supported by a programme of Continuing Professional Development (CPD).

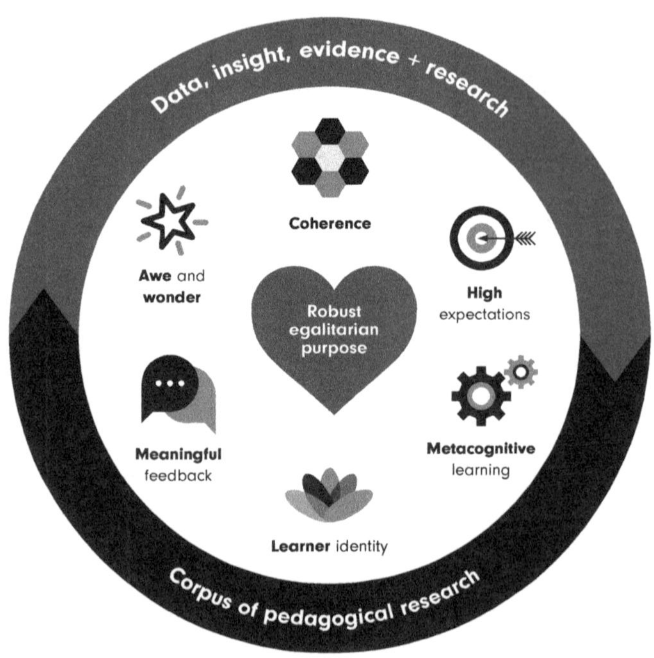

Quest and the six pillars

The six core curriculum pillars that underpin *Oxford Smart* English are as follows:

Pillar 1: Provide clear and coherent curriculum pathways

Quest provides a coherent learning structure by using a broad range of texts and topics which build towards GCSE, providing links to key themes in the set texts and poetry. Chapter 1 *Texts all around us* in Student Book 1, lays the foundations for what students will encounter throughout the rest of the course, introducing key concepts linked to a range of genres and text types. The knowledge features in the Student Book ensure students understand what they are learning and the skills activities enable them to apply their knowledge. The alternative texts and activities in the worksheets on Kerboodle allow for choice within the curriculum pathway, whilst still delivering the core skills and knowledge.

Pillar 2: Hold equally high expectations, aspirations and ambitions for all learners

Quest introduces students to challenging texts, topics and ideas in an accessible way through its thematic approach. It focuses on English as a discipline, building on learning from KS2 but focusing on what is different about English at KS3. The regular, low-stake quizzes at the end of each unit help teachers identify misconceptions and gaps in understanding, and the additional source texts in the worksheets on Kerboodle can be used for support or challenge.

Pillar 3: Enable responsive teaching and learning that continually evolves and improves

Throughout Quest, skills and knowledge are revisited in fresh and different ways, and in different contexts, to help with intervention and to enable teachers to support students where needed. Activities build carefully and are scaffolded within each unit to help identify where students might need additional support. After each unit of work in the Student Book, students' knowledge will be tested through a mini-checkpoint quiz and next steps will be automatically generated to support or extend their learning. The units of work build to half-termly checkpoint assessments that allow students to apply their knowledge and put their skills into practice. Additional spelling, grammar and punctuation quizzes will also help to target misconceptions, gaps in learning and areas that need more explicit teaching.

Pillar 4: Support engaged, self-regulated and metacognitive learning

Metacognitive strategies are embedded throughout the units of the Student Book to promote student independence and develop self-regulated learners, with guidance and ideas about additional overviews in the Teacher Book. The chapter openers will activate prior knowledge, while the learning journeys give students a clear pathway of what and how they will be learning and why. Additional information and support for embedding metacognition is provided as part of the CPD and Research Hub on Kerboodle.

Pillar 5: Promote development of learner identity and identification with curriculum content

The topics in Quest have been carefully chosen for their relevance to students. The Student Book and Kerboodle resources include texts from contemporary and classic writers from a range of backgrounds, cultures and experiences. The alternative texts in the worksheets on Kerboodle allow teachers to tailor their lessons to a particular group of students. Activities throughout the resources encourage students to draw on their own contexts, knowledge and ideas to develop their reading, writing, speaking and listening identities.

Pillar 6: Stimulate fascination, awe and wonder in discovery of self and the world around us

The units in Quest introduce students to engaging themes, big ideas and key concepts that will encourage and stimulate debate and engage learners. The source texts have been chosen in order to unlock new worlds and offer insights into alternative experiences and, along with the themes and topics covered, will help students to build their hinterland knowledge and discovery of self. There are also suggestions for class readers and further reading to help expand students' knowledge and boost their wider understanding of texts and the world around them.

More information on each pillar can be found in the CPD and Research Hub on Kerboodle.

Overview of Quest

Quest comprises digital and printed Student Books and Teacher Books for each year of KS3, digital worksheets to support the Student Book, assessment resources, and research and professional development resources. The course aligns to the skills and knowledge set out in the National Curriculum for KS3 and is underpinned by the six pillars of the *Oxford Smart* Curriculum Service. Content is delivered through engaging topics, each of which explores 'big ideas' to help students understand what they need to learn and why, and to encourage and stimulate debate and ideas.

Students will cover nine topics, one per term. Topics and texts have been chosen because they are engaging, relevant and inspiring. They will also lay the foundations for the types of texts and themes that students will study at KS4, helping to prepare them for their GCSE course.

Each chapter has a theme and poses and answers key questions:

	1 Texts all around us	2 Crime and consequences	3 Journeys and discoveries
Year 7	• What is a text? • How have language and texts evolved over time? • Whose voices have been heard and how can you use your voice today?	• What lies behind readers' fascination with crime? • How has crime writing changed over time? • What makes a great detective?	• How have stories of journeys of discovery shaped English literature? • How is character revealed by the challenges and dangers faced? • Why do we undertake journeys? How can they help us to better understand ourselves?

	1 Influence and power	2 Terror and wonder	3 Wild places and urban landscapes
Year 8	• Do your decisions rely on your emotions or your intelligence? • How do writers appeal to a reader's emotions when they attempt to influence or persuade? • Who are the influencers – both now and in the past?	• How does fear fuel the imagination? • Are terror and wonder two sides of the same coin? • How has Gothic fiction shaped English literature over the past 250 years?	• How have different environments inspired writers' imaginations? • How have writers expressed ideas about the relationship between humans and their environment? • How do writers explore the spaces in between?

	1 Truth and lies	2 Utopia and dystopia	3 Youth and age
Year 9	• What is the news and what makes a good journalist? • How can we tell truth from lies? • How has the way news is gathered and distributed affected language use, presentation and objectivity?	• Can the perfect society ever exist? • Is one person's utopia another person's dystopia? • How have utopias and dystopias been depicted in fiction?	• Does age bring wisdom or do the young see the world more clearly? • How do writers comment on adult experiences through the more innocent eyes of a child? • How has the 'coming-of-age' genre developed over time?

Texts

Throughout Quest, students will encounter a wide variety of texts from different authors, genres, forms (written and spoken) and time periods that:

- will develop and empower them as readers, writers and communicators
- are from writers who reflect, challenge and broaden students' identities and experiences
- cover a broad variety of topics and themes
- are diverse and representative
- unlock new worlds and offer insights into their own experiences
- build their background knowledge and self-discovery
- are high-quality and appropriate for study

Quest pathways

<table>
<tr><th>Core curriculum pathway</th><th>Alternative curriculum pathway</th><th>Assessment</th><th>Planning and delivery</th><th>CPD</th></tr>
<tr><th>Student Book</th><th>Kerboodle</th><th>Kerboodle</th><th>Teacher Book and Kerboodle</th><th>Kerboodle</th></tr>
<tr><td>Chapter 1: Texts all around us
Units 1–4</td><td rowspan="2">Alternative source texts and activities for each unit, delivering the same learning outcomes</td><td rowspan="2">Mini-checkpoint quizzes at the end of each unit to review students' knowledge.
Checkpoint assessments to assess students, application of their knowledge, using their reading, writing or speaking and listening skills after Units 4 and 8.
Spelling, grammar and punctuation quizzes to be used as a diagnostic tool or as a learning review tool after a specific grammar lesson.</td><td rowspan="6">Long-term plans
Medium-term chapter plans
Short-term unit plans
Lesson delivery support: teacher notes and slides</td><td rowspan="6">Course and subject delivery support
English subject knowledge and pedagogy</td></tr>
<tr><td>Chapter 1: Texts all around us
Units 5–8</td></tr>
<tr><td>Chapter 2: Crime and consequences
Units 1–4</td><td rowspan="2">Alternative source texts and activities for each unit, delivering the same learning outcomes</td><td rowspan="2">Mini-checkpoint quizzes at the end of each unit to review students' knowledge.
Checkpoint assessments to assess students, application of their knowledge, using their reading, writing or speaking and listening skills after Units 4 and 8.
Spelling, grammar and punctuation quizzes to be used as a diagnostic tool or as a learning review tool after a specific grammar lesson.</td></tr>
<tr><td>Chapter 2: Crime and consequences
Units 5–8</td></tr>
<tr><td>Chapter 3: Journeys and discoveries
Units 1–4</td><td rowspan="2">Alternative source texts and activities for each unit, delivering the same learning outcomes</td><td rowspan="2">Mini-checkpoint quizzes at the end of each unit to review students' knowledge.
Checkpoint assessments to assess students, application of their knowledge, using their reading, writing or speaking and listening skills after Units 4 and 8.
Spelling, grammar and punctuation quizzes to be used as a diagnostic tool or as a learning review tool after a specific grammar lesson.</td></tr>
<tr><td>Chapter 3: Journeys and discoveries
Units 5–8</td></tr>
</table>

The core pathway

The core pathway is delivered through the Student Book. The Student Book has three chapters, each covering one big theme.

Each chapter has eight units of work, grouped into two parts. Each part has a different focus, e.g. Units 1–4 might cover fiction and Units 5–8 might be on non-fiction. Each individual unit also has a particular skills focus: reading, writing or speaking and listening.

A unit will take approximately two or three lessons, depending on how it is taught. This makes the course flexible enough to fit into a school's timetable and to allow for a more personalised approach to teaching and learning.

Alternative pathway

There are additional source texts and activities on Kerboodle, offering a choice of resources that can be selected as appropriate for particular students.

Using the Quest Student Book

Student Books 1, 2 and 3 correspond to the three years at KS3. The first unit in Student Book 1 builds on the knowledge students have from KS2 and introduces a variety of texts that they experience in their lives and then looks at specific text types and themes. Books 2 and 3 develop students' knowledge and skills further and prepare them for English at KS4.

Each chapter in the Student Book starts with a chapter opener that activates prior knowledge and informs students about what they will be learning.

The learning overview supports metacognition by preparing students for what they will be learning and will help them to monitor what they have learned. It also shows a coherent learning pathway through the Student Book.

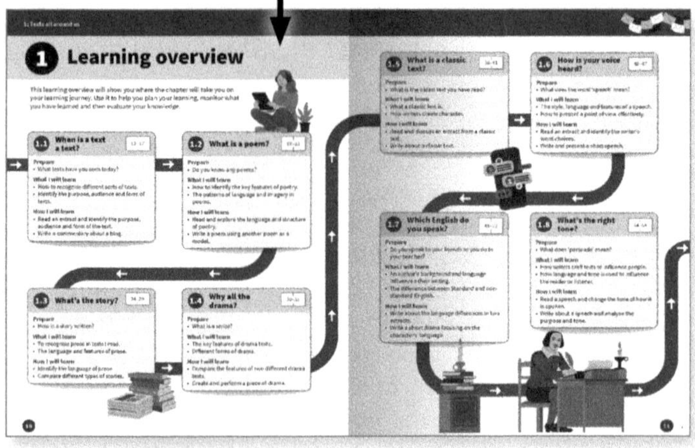

Big idea: gives an overview of what the unit is about and why it is important. It can also include links to previous units as a reminder of what students already know.

Tips: remind students of a connection to another key piece of knowledge or key skill, and give prompts.

Learning objectives: focus on what students will be learning and how they will demonstrate their understanding. The first objective is about what students will learn, the second is about what they are exploring, investigating or considering further, and the third objective is to write, analyse or present what they have learned.

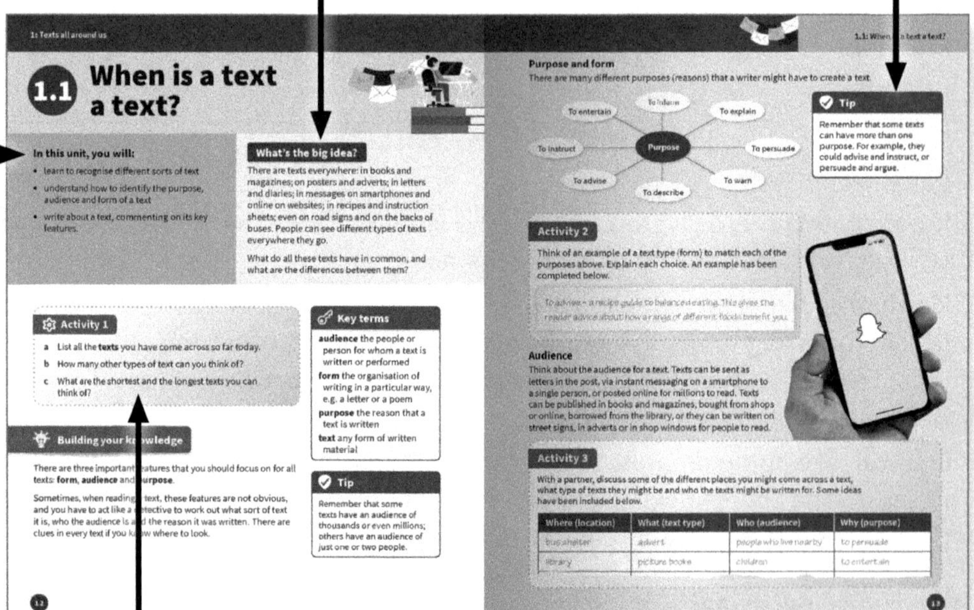

Metacognitive activities: require students to think about what they already know about the text, the theme or the skills they'll be using.

Boosting your vocabulary: activities and strategies to help students work out unfamiliar words, along with opportunities for them to practise using the words in their own writing.

Building your knowledge: introduces the knowledge focus of the unit in the context of the source text. Students are encouraged to think about what they already know and understand about the focus of the unit, drawing on their own experiences.

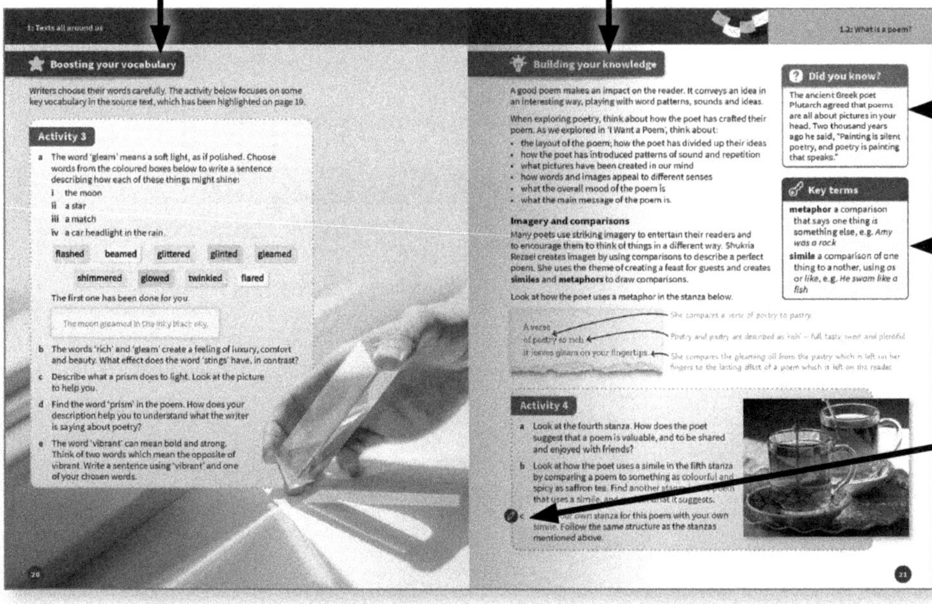

Did you know?: offers short and snappy facts to aid or add to students' comprehension of a text.

Key terms: are flagged the first time they appear in a chapter and include technical or literary terms.

Writing icon: shows when students are expected to write their answer or response to the activity. All other parts of the activity can be used to prompt a discussion or a whole-class written response.

Putting it all together: all of the tasks in the unit build towards students completing an activity that will allow them to demonstrate they have understood the skills and knowledge covered.

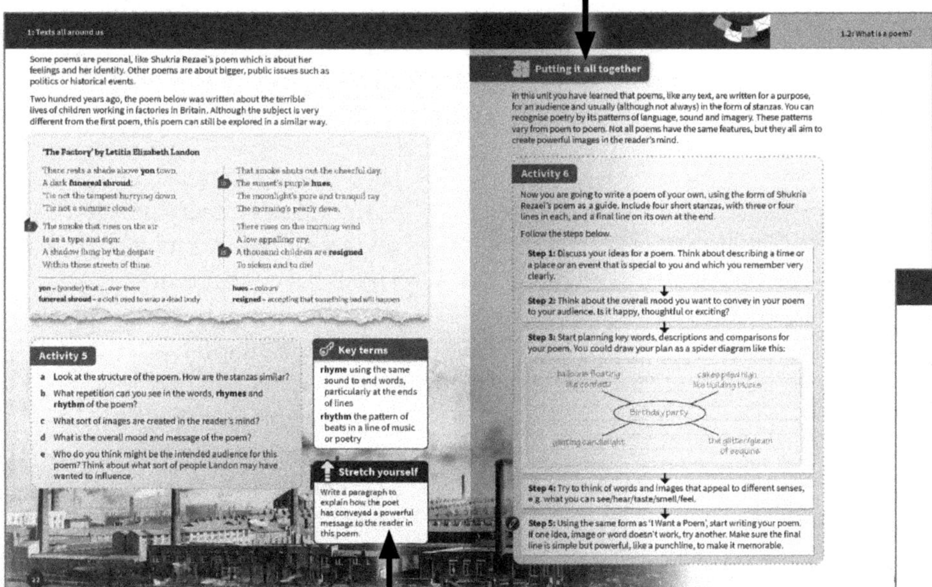

Modelled answers: can be used to support students with their own writing or responses.

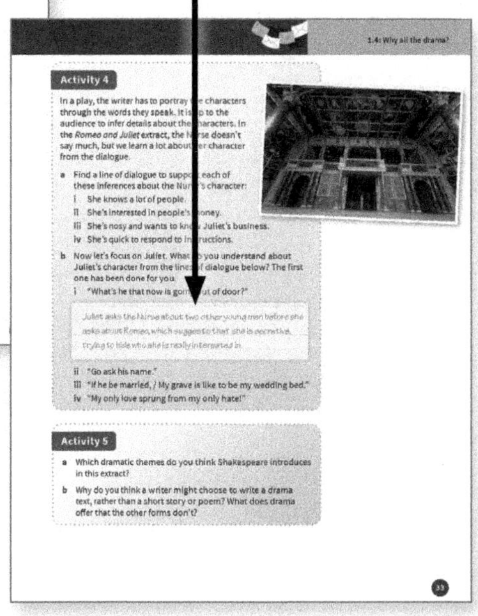

Stretch yourself: activities encourage students to think in more depth or to take their learning further in order to expand their knowledge and develop their skills.

Using the Quest Teacher Book

The Teacher Book supports the planning and implementation of Quest, using the Quest Student Book and Kerboodle resources. For every chapter of Quest, the Teacher Book contains:

- an introduction to the topic
- guidance on how to use the chapter openers
- unit-by-unit overviews with flexible lesson activities.

The chapter overview grid outlines the eight units: the skills focus, source texts, alternative source texts on Kerboodle and objectives.

The chapter introduction includes icons linked to the *Oxford Smart* curriculum pillars, showing how the pillars have been embedded into Quest.

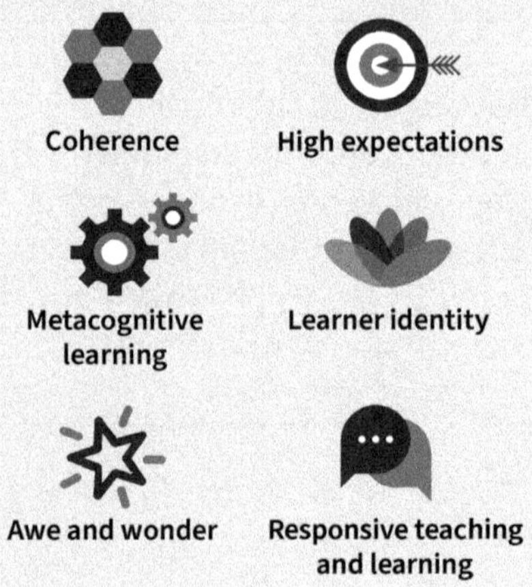

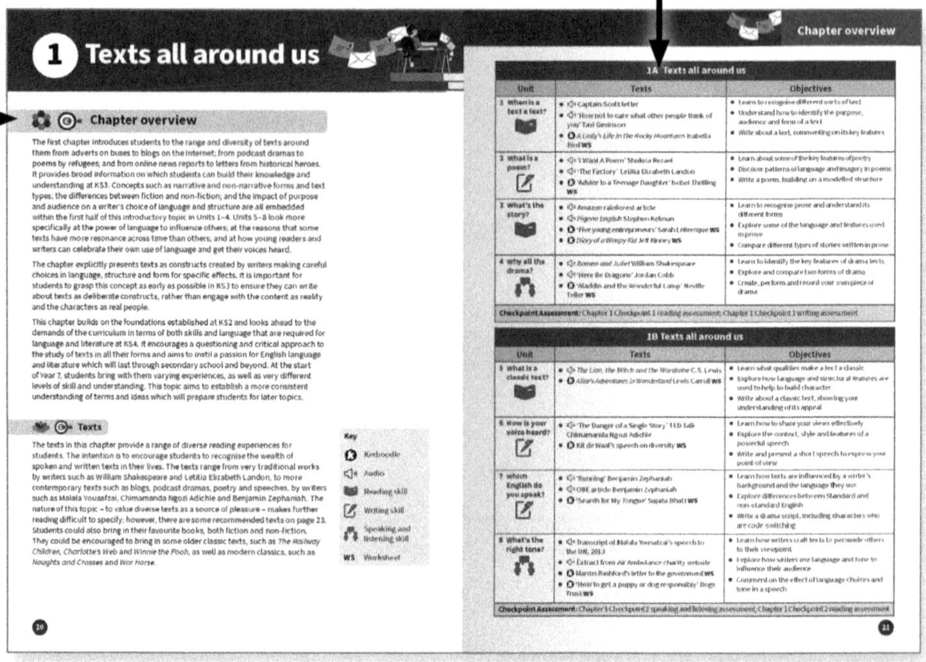

These pages help to explain the chapter and the topic in more detail, giving guidance on making cross-curricular links and building students' background knowledge.

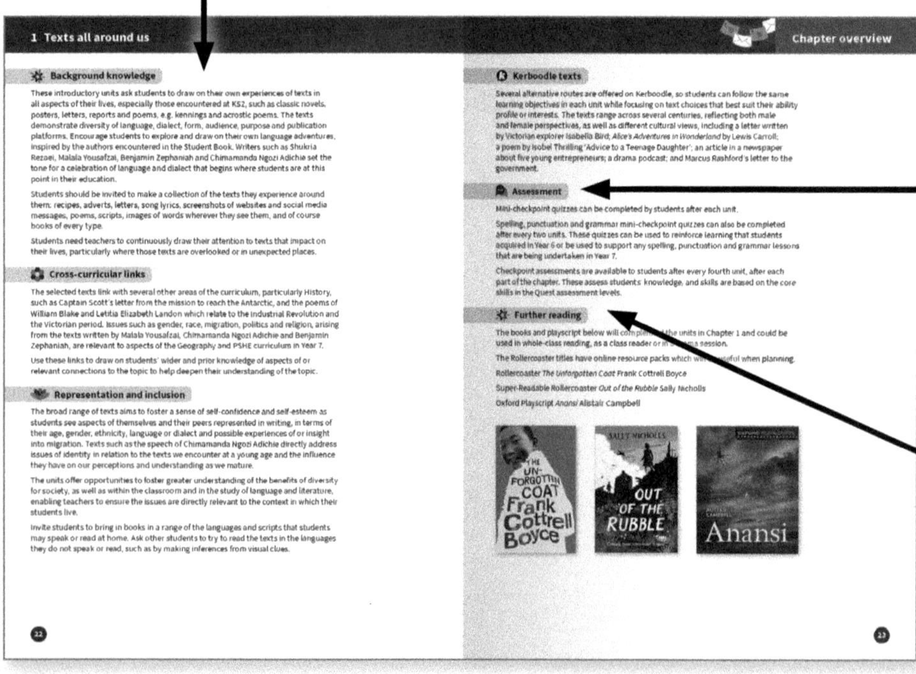

Mini-checkpoints can be assigned after every unit to review students' knowledge. There are checkpoint assessments at the end of each part of the chapter, after Units 4 and 8. Spelling, grammar and punctuation quizzes can also be used to support lessons or individual students as needed. Please refer to pages 16–17 for more information on assessment in Quest.

Suggestions for further reading, either for class novels and playscripts, or for students to read on their own, are included in every chapter.

This is guidance on how to use the Student Book chapter openers. These openers help to engage students with the topic of the chapter, to show them what they will be learning and to activate prior learning. The information on these pages will help to guide students in completing the metacognitive activities that will support their understanding of the learning in the Student Book.

Key vocabulary links to the theme and will help to support students in accessing the texts.

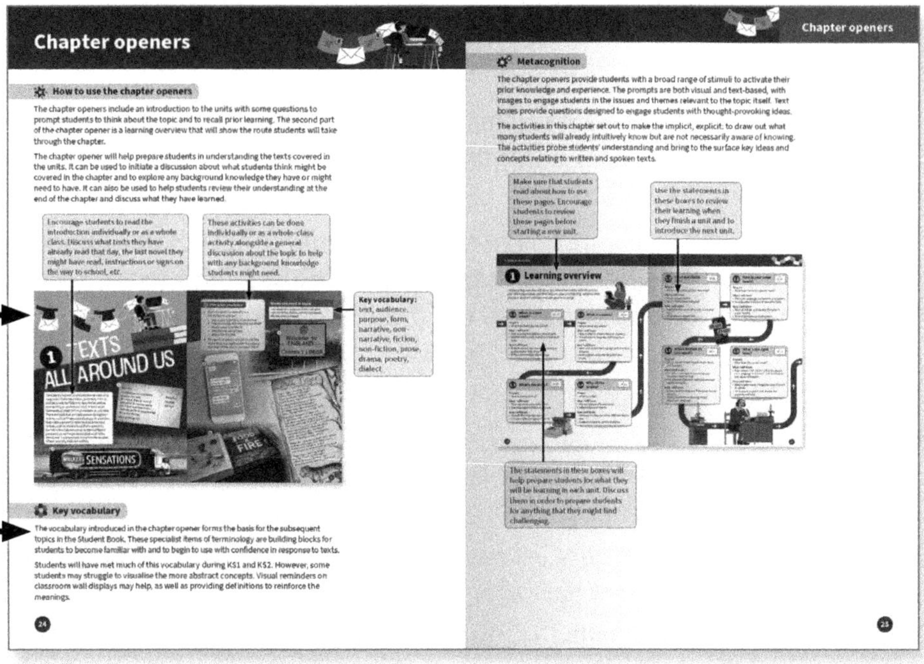

The unit focus offers an overview of objectives, texts and key terms covered in that unit. Before starting, it may help to spend time explaining the key terms to make sure that students are familiar with them before they encounter them in the unit.

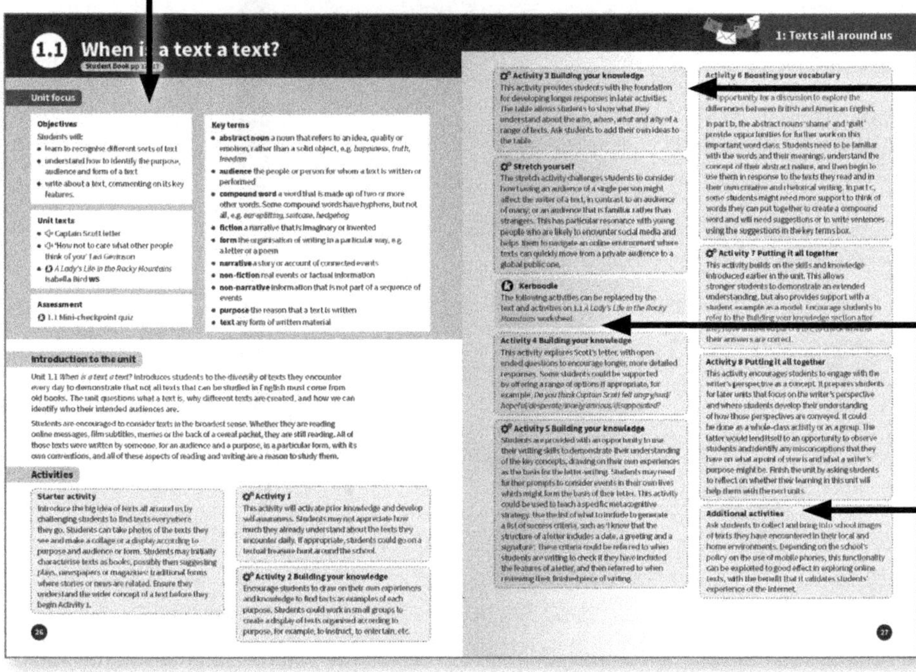

The activities follow the sequence of the Student Book and support the learning with guidance on implementation, metacognitive strategies, support and extension ideas and possible homework activities.

This box indicates where the alternative text provided on Kerboodle could be used rather than the source text in the Student Book.

There are additional activities that can be used to support, extend or for homework.

Kerboodle

Oxford Smart Quest Kerboodle provides additional teaching and learning resources, as well as a comprehensive assessment package. Resources include worksheets with alternative texts, audio, automatically marked assessments, books, and the CPD and Research Hub.

Kerboodle is online, allowing teachers and students to access the course anytime and anywhere. Homework and assessments can be set through the Assessment system and progress can be tracked using the Markbook.

Kerboodle book

The *Oxford Smart* Quest Kerboodle book provides a digital copy of the Student Book for use at the front of the classroom or for students to access independently.

Teacher access to the Kerboodle book is automatically available as part of the Resources and Assessment package.

A set of tools is available with the Kerboodle book, allowing teachers to personalise their book and make notes.

Like all other resources offered on Kerboodle, the Kerboodle book can be accessed on a range of devices.

Use different tools such as sticky notes, bookmarks and pen features to personalise each page.

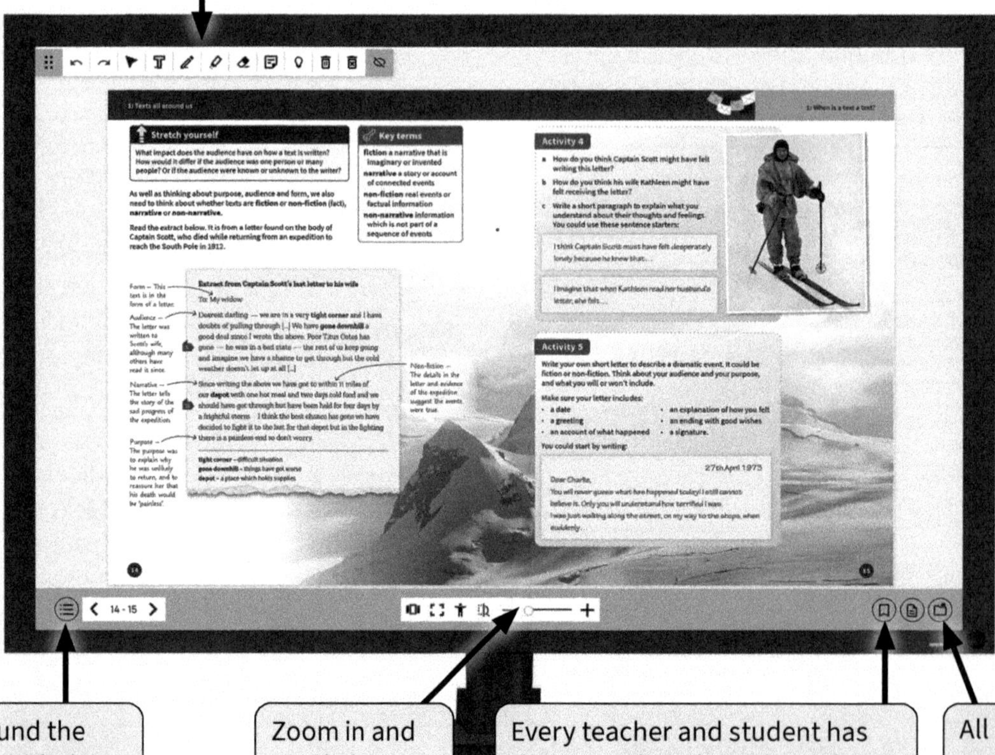

Navigate around the book quickly with the contents menu, key word search or page number search.

Zoom in and spotlight text.

Every teacher and student has their own digital notebook for use within their Kerboodle book. You can choose to share your notes with students or hide them from view – all student notes are accessible to themselves only.

All the associated resources can be viewed on each spread.

Resources

Click the Resources tab to access the full list of *Oxford Smart* Quest lesson resources. The resources section includes:

- documents containing the texts from the Student Book
- audio recordings of all the text extracts from the Student Book
- PowerPoint slides to help with lesson delivery
- lesson notes for use when teaching – these are a version of what's in the Teacher Book
- worksheets containing additional texts to replace or supplement the source texts in the Student Book.

Resources matching every lesson in the *Oxford Smart* Quest series are shown here.

Set single or multiple assignments for your classes using the Assignment basket.

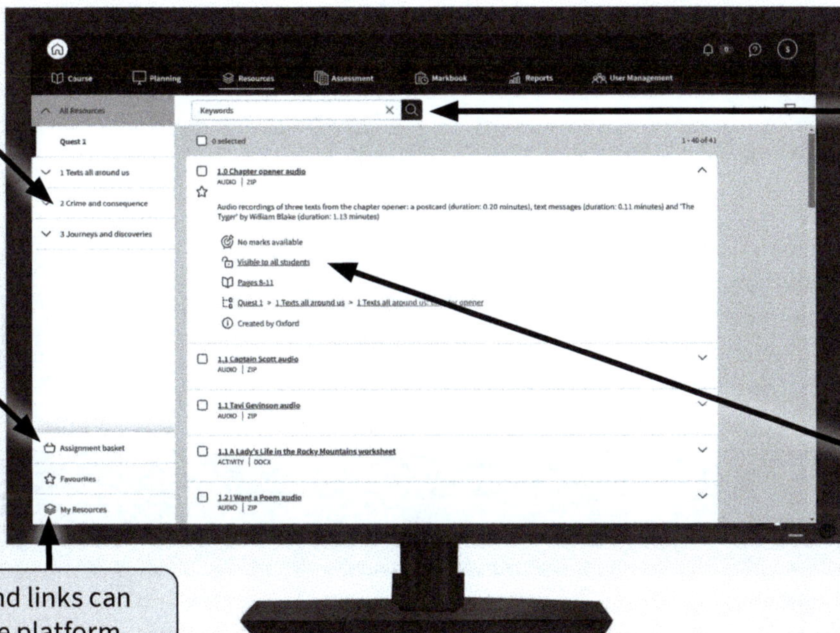

Navigation panel and search bar allow for easy navigation between resources by book, unit and chapter.

Resources can be made visible to or hidden from students and a link will take you to the corresponding Student Book spread.

Existing resources and links can be uploaded onto the platform using the My Resources section.

Worksheets and alternative texts

These alternative texts provide a flexible approach to teaching the objectives for the unit, allowing the teacher to tailor the curriculum to different needs: more accessible and relevant texts, challenging texts and more diversity.

Guidance in the Teacher Book indicates where the alternative text can replace the source text in the Student Book.

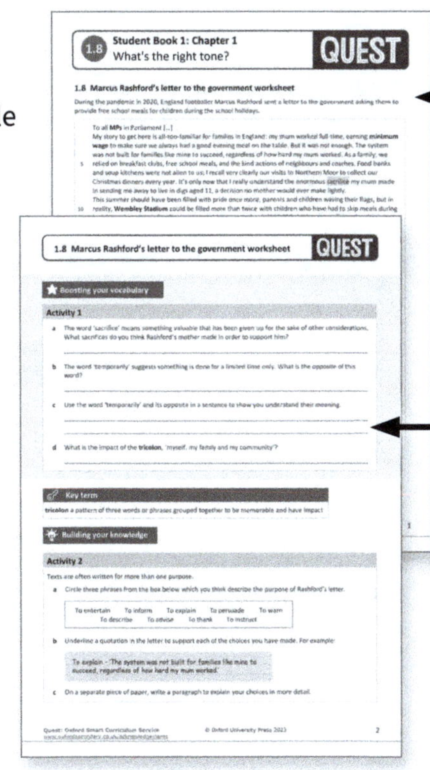

The worksheets contain the same types of activities that are in the Student Book.

Students can write directly onto the worksheets.

Kerboodle

Assessment and Markbook

All the assessment material on Kerboodle has been developed alongside the curriculum and resources. Clicking on the Assessment tab will reveal a range of materials to help deliver a varied, motivating and effective assessment programme.

It is easy to import class registers and create user accounts for students. Once the class is set up, assessments can be assigned for students to do individually or as a group. They can also complete them at home.

The Markbook with a reporting function helps to keep track of students' results. This includes both automarked assessment and work that needs to be teacher-marked.

You can find out more about the Assessment framework on page 17.

In the Assessment tab, you can find mini-checkpoints for each lesson, checkpoints for each chapter and end-of-unit assessments for each unit.

The Markbook and reporting function helps you track your students' progress.

Reports can be generated using data from the checkpoints and mini-checkpoints.

Different follow-up tasks are available to students after they complete the checkpoints and mini-checkpoints, depending on how well they did.

Kerboodle Research Library

The Research Library contains:

- the pedagogical research and evidence that have been drawn on when developing the Quest resources, as well as more information on the *Oxford Smart* Curriculum and the six pillars that underpin it
- summaries of other wider pedagogical research that impacts the current and future classroom, such as vocabulary and word gap reports, the various aspects of reading, oracy, grammar and metacognition.

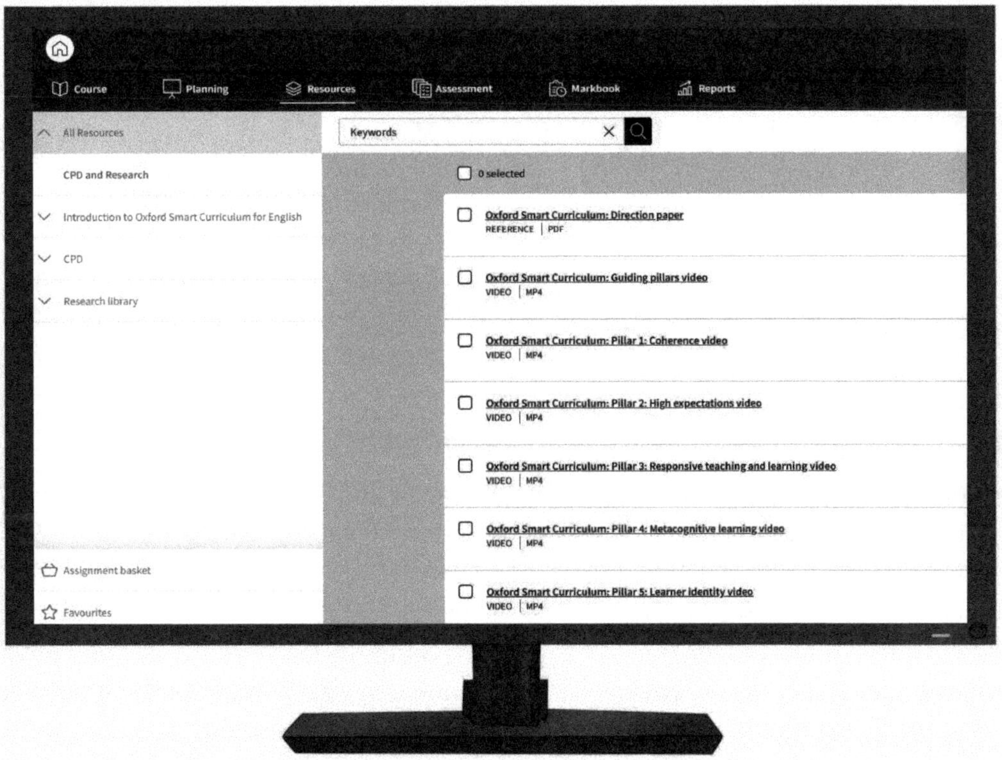

Continuing professional development

Alongside the Research Library, CPD resources will support implementation of Quest.

These resources include blogs, articles and videos and will be delivered in easy-to-access modules that can be undertaken by individuals or groups, depending on how each school plans and delivers their CPD sessions. The resources will cover the pillars of the *Oxford Smart* Curriculum, how to use the Quest resources in the classroom, and other relevant topics, such as vocabulary and oracy.

Impact

The extensive testing of Quest within pioneer schools has informed the content of the course. This link to schools and future research will help continually update and review Quest to provide an up-to-date and relevant course.

The Research Library will also continue to be updated as the body of research grows to support the implementation of effective pedagogy in the classroom.

Assessment

Quest's assessment model combines regular formative and summative assessments along with low-stakes quizzing that aims to interrupt the forgetting curve and ensures that students have grasped key concepts.

Student Book 1 example assessment journey

	Chapter								End of year
	Unit 1	Unit 2	Unit 3	Unit 4	Unit 5	Unit 6	Unit 7	Unit 8	
Mini-checkpoints	✓	✓	✓	✓	✓	✓	✓	✓	
Checkpoints				✓				✓	
Reactivate quizzes	Triggered by mini-checkpoints								
End of year assessment									✓

Mini-checkpoints

These automarked quizzes at the end of each unit of the Student Book will test that students have acquired and understood the knowledge introduced in that unit.

Following each mini-checkpoint, students will be presented with a personalised next step that will either support them to achieve 'secure', or provide challenge questions to reach 'extending'.

Additional grammar, punctuation and spelling quizzes throughout Quest target areas that need more explicit teaching, misconceptions or gaps in learning.

Reactivate quizzes

These automarked retrieval quizzes will be automatically triggered each time a student completes a mini-checkpoint quiz, and will recap the knowledge that students have covered.

Checkpoints

Units of work in the Student Book will build to half-termly checkpoint assessments that allow students to put their skills into practice. These checkpoints will follow the assessment framework developed for *Oxford Smart* Curriculum for English (available on Kerboodle), allowing teachers to assess, record and track the progress of all students across the nine chapters in the core skills of reading, writing, and speaking and listening.

Tracking progress

The mini-checkpoint quizzes and half-termly checkpoint assessments will help to identify and assess where students are developing, secure and extending their knowledge and skills.

- Developing: learners are working towards secure knowledge and understanding but need more support to achieve this.
- Secure: learners have a secure knowledge and understanding; this is the aspiration for all learners to achieve, prior to moving on to the next topic.
- Extending: learners are working beyond age-related expectation, and their knowledge and understanding can be stretched and challenged.

Assessment descriptors

Reading	Retrieval (R1)	Retrieve and summarise information and ideas from texts; select appropriate references and use these references to support a point of view.
	Interpretation (R2)	Understand ideas and perspectives in texts; make inferences and interpretations; identify and interpret the context of texts. Evaluate the significance of texts.
	Methods (R3)	Understand that texts are deliberate constructs; explore the effects of the methods writers use to create texts; comment on and evaluate the impact of methods on the text as a whole, using a range of subject terms appropriately.
	Comparison (R4)	Make links between information and ideas from different texts; comment on and evaluate the relationships between texts. Compare writers' perspectives in different texts, including how writers use different methods for different purposes and audiences.

Writing	Communicating ideas (W1)	Generate, select and develop ideas; communicate ideas and perspectives effectively using different forms and genres. Write engagingly for different purposes and audiences.
	Structure and organisation (W2)	Plan, draft and organise writing effectively, using cohesive sentences and paragraphs, sequencing and developing ideas coherently and using a range of structural features.
	Crafting (W3)	Create texts using varied tone, style and register and using vocabulary accurately and appropriately. Craft writing using a range of linguistic methods to produce increasingly complex texts using a range of rhetorical and narrative methods.
	Accuracy (W4)	Use sentence forms to create impact and punctuation to convey meaning. Spell increasingly complex words accurately and use grammatical constructions in a controlled way.

Speaking and listening	Voice (S1)	Speak audibly and confidently in a range of situations, varying the pace and tone of speaking. Project voice to engage an audience and use body language and facial expression appropriately.
	Vocabulary (S2)	Use an appropriate range of vocabulary and grammatical constructions when talking, adopting an appropriate register and/or style for audience and purpose. Use rhetorical/linguistic techniques appropriate to the task.
	Organisation (S3)	Plan and structure talk effectively for a range of audiences and purposes, using a range of methods, maintaining focus and managing time. Monitor and continually evaluate the impact of talk.
	Collaboration (S4)	Take turns when talking and manage interactions, listening actively and responding appropriately. Use questions to seek information and clarification and give reasons to support own views and to build on or challenge others' contributions.

End of year assessment

At the end of each year there will be a summative assessment, available either as a digital or paper-based assessment.

Metacognition

What is metacognition?

To help students become increasingly independent and confident learners, teachers need to facilitate students' understanding of their own strengths and weaknesses and the strategies that they use to learn. Metacognition is about teaching students to be strategic learners. A metacognitive learner may consider their motivation towards learning and how this impacts their effort and progress; they may consciously plan how to approach a task, monitor how it's going, and evaluate how they can improve on their learning in the future. Metacognitive learners are supported by teachers to set their own meaningful goals, identify and utilise the strategies that work for them, and self-reflect on their effectiveness. Teachers can enable learners to become more metacognitive through: their approach to planning and delivering lessons; developing a growth mindset in students; making explicit the learning processes they themselves go through as 'experts', so that students can see how to progress. There are many strategies teachers can employ to improve the metacognition of learners in their classroom and this guide aims to:

- introduce the Plan, Monitor, Evaluate (PME) cycle
- support teachers with understanding the seven stages of developing metacognition explicitly as developed by the Education Endowment Foundation (EEF).

The Plan, Monitor, Evaluate (PME) cycle

The Plan, Monitor, Evaluate (PME) cycle is a core part of metacognition and helps students regulate their learning by building their knowledge of themselves as learners and of specific strategies or tasks. This cycle forms a structured reflection process that students can follow when completing a task or undertaking independent study.

1 **Planning (before the task):** During this phase of the cycle, students think about the goal of the task ahead, reflecting on the subject knowledge required, and whether specific strategies need to be used. They should consider things like whether they have done a similar task before and whether they have experience that they can use to be successful now.

2 **Monitoring (during the task):** During this phase, students review their progress against the goals of the task. This could mean that they reflect on whether their chosen strategy is successful and make any necessary changes.

3 **Evaluation (end of the task):** During this phase, students evaluate the effectiveness of their plan. They can review the strengths and weaknesses of what they produced and reflect on whether they would do anything differently next time.

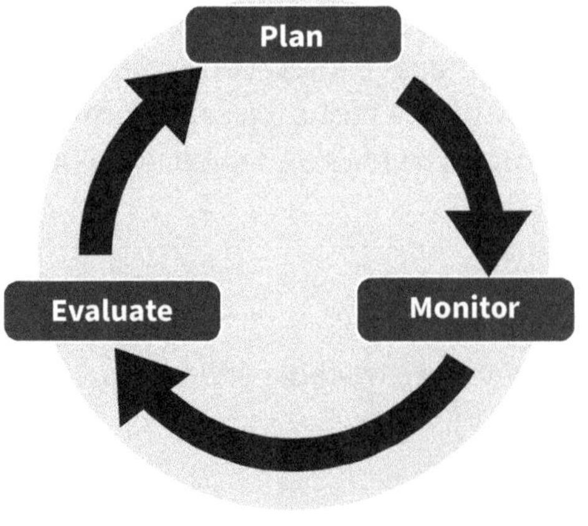

Teaching the PME cycle

One way to approach teaching this is to use a regulatory checklist. This is a series of questions that guide students through each phase. These questions can be introduced to students so that they understand why the PME cycle is effective and how they can use it. In practice, it may be more appropriate to focus on one of the phases first, rather than the whole checklist, or to have the whole class reflect on the questions as a group, rather than individually. Over time, through guided practice, students will become more independent, leading to the PME cycle naturally becoming the way that they approach new tasks.

Planning

- What are your starting points for learning?
- What do you already know about the theme/genre/skill/ feature?
- How confident do you feel about an activity or text?
- Do you need to recap anything?
- What similar tasks have been completed previously? What strategies worked well and what could be improved?
- Have you got or are you going to plan any success criteria?

Monitoring

- What could you do to check your work and improve it?
- How confident are you with the task?
- Is the strategy you are using working?
- How do you know that the strategy is working?
- Is your answer meeting the success criteria?

Evaluation

- What went well?
- What strategies worked successfully?
- What might you change for next time?
- What do you still need to know?
- What knowledge would have made this better?
- What could you do to meet any particular success criteria?

The EEF seven-step guide

The Education Endowment Foundation suggests following the seven-step approach to teaching metacognitive skills. This seven-step approach can be used as a planning tool to support the delivery of any new skill or strategy, and can be used in all aspects of learning.

1 Activate prior knowledge
2 Explicit strategy instruction
3 Modelling of learned strategy
4 Memorisation of strategy
5 Guided practice
6 Independent practice
7 Structured reflection

Metacognition in Quest

Metacognitive activities are indicated in both the Student Book and Teacher Book with an icon, so it is easy to see when metacognition is being covered.

The icon in the Teacher Book reflects the links of the *Oxford Smart* Curriculum to pillar 4: support engaged, self-regulated and metacognitive learning. It indicates that, in that part of the Student Book, students are learning or being encouraged to use metacognitive strategies.

The icon in the Student Book indicates where an activity is using a metacognitive strategy.

1 Texts all around us

Chapter overview

The first chapter introduces students to the range and diversity of texts around them from adverts on buses to blogs on the Internet; from podcast dramas to poems by refugees; and from online news reports to letters from historical heroes. It provides broad information on which students can build their knowledge and understanding at KS3. Concepts such as narrative and non-narrative forms and text types; the differences between fiction and non-fiction; and the impact of purpose and audience on a writer's choice of language and structure are all embedded within the first half of this introductory topic in Units 1–4. Units 5–8 look more specifically at the power of language to influence others; at the reasons that some texts have more resonance across time than others; and at how young readers and writers can celebrate their own use of language and get their voices heard.

The chapter explicitly presents texts as constructs created by writers making careful choices in language, structure and form for specific effects. It is important for students to grasp this concept as early as possible in KS3 to ensure they can write about texts as deliberate constructs, rather than engage with the content as reality and the characters as real people.

This chapter builds on the foundations established at KS2 and looks ahead to the demands of the curriculum in terms of both skills and language that are required for language and literature at KS4. It encourages a questioning and critical approach to the study of texts in all their forms and aims to instil a passion for English language and literature which will last through secondary school and beyond. At the start of Year 7, students bring with them varying experiences, as well as very different levels of skill and understanding. This topic aims to establish a more consistent understanding of terms and ideas which will prepare students for later topics.

Texts

The texts in this chapter provide a range of diverse reading experiences for students. The intention is to encourage students to recognise the wealth of spoken and written texts in their lives. The texts range from very traditional works by writers such as William Shakespeare and Letitia Elizabeth Landon, to more contemporary texts such as blogs, podcast dramas, poetry and speeches, by writers such as Malala Yousafzai, Chimamanda Ngozi Adichie and Benjamin Zephaniah. The nature of this topic – to value diverse texts as a source of pleasure – makes further reading difficult to specify; however, there are some recommended texts on page 23. Students could also bring in their favourite books, both fiction and non-fiction. They could be encouraged to bring in some older classic texts, such as *The Railway Children, Charlotte's Web* and *Winnie the Pooh*, as well as modern classics, such as *Noughts and Crosses* and *War Horse*.

Key

- Kerboodle
- Audio
- Reading skill
- Writing skill
- Speaking and listening skill
- **WS** Worksheet

1A Texts all around us		
Unit	**Texts**	**Objectives**
1 When is a text a text?	• Captain Scott letter • 'How not to care what other people think of you' Tavi Gevinson • *A Lady's Life in the Rocky Mountains* Isabella Bird **WS**	• Learn to recognise different sorts of text • Understand how to identify the purpose, audience and form of a text • Write about a text, commenting on its key features
2 What is a poem?	• 'I Want A Poem' Shukria Rezaei • 'The Factory' Letitia Elizabeth Landon • 'Advice to a Teenage Daughter' Isobel Thrilling **WS**	• Learn about some of the key features of poetry • Discover patterns of language and imagery in poems • Write a poem, building on a modelled structure
3 What's the story?	• Amazon rainforest article • *Pigeon English* Stephen Kelman • 'Five young entrepreneurs' Sarah LeBrecque **WS** • *Diary of a Wimpy Kid* Jeff Kinney **WS**	• Learn to recognise prose and understand its different forms • Explore some of the language and features used in prose • Compare different types of stories written in prose
4 Why all the drama?	• *Romeo and Juliet* William Shakespeare • 'Here Be Dragons' Jordan Cobb • 'Aladdin and the Wonderful Lamp' Neville Teller **WS**	• Learn to identify the key features of drama texts • Explore and compare two forms of drama • Create, perform and record your own piece of drama
Checkpoint Assessment: Chapter 1 Checkpoint 1 reading assessment; Chapter 1 Checkpoint 1 writing assessment		

1B Texts all around us		
Unit	**Texts**	**Objectives**
5 What is a classic text?	• *The Lion, the Witch and the Wardrobe* C.S. Lewis • *Alice's Adventures in Wonderland* Lewis Carroll **WS**	• Learn what qualities make a text a classic • Explore how language and structural features are used to help to build character • Write about a classic text, showing your understanding of its appeal
6 How is your voice heard?	• 'The Danger of a Single Story' TED Talk Chimamanda Ngozi Adichie • Kit de Waal's speech on diversity **WS**	• Learn how to share your views effectively • Explore the context, style and features of a powerful speech • Write and present a short speech to express your point of view
7 Which English do you speak?	• 'Running' Benjamin Zephaniah • OBE article Benjamin Zephaniah • 'Search for My Tongue' Sujata Bhatt **WS**	• Learn how texts are influenced by a writer's background and the language they use • Explore differences between Standard and non-standard English • Write a drama script, including characters who are code-switching
8 What's the right tone?	• Transcript of Malala Yousafzai's speech to the UN, 2013 • Extract from Air Ambulance charity website • Marcus Rashford's letter to the government **WS** • 'How to get a puppy or dog responsibly' Dogs Trust **WS**	• Learn how writers craft texts to persuade others to their viewpoint • Explore how writers use language and tone to influence their audience • Comment on the effect of language choices and tone in a speech
Checkpoint Assessment: Chapter 1 Checkpoint 2 speaking and listening assessment; Chapter 1 Checkpoint 2 reading assessment		

Background knowledge

These introductory units ask students to draw on their own experiences of texts in all aspects of their lives, especially those encountered at KS2, such as classic novels, posters, letters, reports and poems, e.g. kennings and acrostic poems. The texts demonstrate diversity of language, dialect, form, audience, purpose and publication platforms. Encourage students to explore and draw on their own language adventures, inspired by the authors encountered in the Student Book. Writers such as Shukria Rezaei, Malala Yousafzai, Benjamin Zephaniah and Chimamanda Ngozi Adichie set the tone for a celebration of language and dialect that begins where students are at this point in their education.

Students should be invited to make a collection of the texts they experience around them: recipes, adverts, letters, song lyrics, screenshots of websites and social media messages, poems, scripts, images of words wherever they see them, and of course books of every type.

Students need teachers to continuously draw their attention to texts that impact on their lives, particularly where those texts are overlooked or in unexpected places.

Cross-curricular links

The selected texts link with several other areas of the curriculum, particularly History, such as Captain Scott's letter from the mission to reach the Antarctic, and the poems of William Blake and Letitia Elizabeth Landon which relate to the Industrial Revolution and the Victorian period. Issues such as gender, race, migration, politics and religion, arising from the texts written by Malala Yousafzai, Chimamanda Ngozi Adichie and Benjamin Zephaniah, are relevant to aspects of the Geography and PSHE curriculum in Year 7.

Use these links to draw on students' wider and prior knowledge of aspects of or relevant connections to the topic to help deepen their understanding of the topic.

Representation and inclusion

The broad range of texts aims to foster a sense of self-confidence and self-esteem as students see aspects of themselves and their peers represented in writing, in terms of their age, gender, ethnicity, language or dialect and possible experiences of or insight into migration. Texts such as the speech of Chimamanda Ngozi Adichie directly address issues of identity in relation to the texts we encounter at a young age and the influence they have on our perceptions and understanding as we mature.

The units offer opportunities to foster greater understanding of the benefits of diversity for society, as well as within the classroom and in the study of language and literature, enabling teachers to ensure the issues are directly relevant to the context in which their students live.

Invite students to bring in books in a range of the languages and scripts that students may speak or read at home. Ask other students to try to read the texts in the languages they do not speak or read, such as by making inferences from visual clues.

Kerboodle texts

Several alternative routes are offered on Kerboodle, so students can follow the same learning objectives in each unit while focusing on text choices that best suit their ability profile or interests. The texts range across several centuries, reflecting both male and female perspectives, as well as different cultural views, including a letter written by Victorian explorer Isabella Bird; *Alice's Adventures in Wonderland* by Lewis Carroll; a poem by Isobel Thrilling 'Advice to a Teenage Daughter'; an article in a newspaper about five young entrepreneurs; a drama podcast; and Marcus Rashford's letter to the government.

Assessment

Mini-checkpoint quizzes can be completed by students after each unit.

Spelling, punctuation and grammar mini-checkpoint quizzes can also be completed after every two units. These quizzes can be used to reinforce learning that students acquired in Year 6 or be used to support any spelling, punctuation and grammar lessons that are being undertaken in Year 7.

Checkpoint assessments are available to students after every fourth unit, after each part of the chapter. These assess students' knowledge, and skills are based on the core skills in the Quest assessment levels.

Further reading

The books and playscript below will complement the units in Chapter 1 and could be used in whole-class reading, as a class reader or in a drama session.

The Rollercoaster titles have online resource packs which will be useful when planning.

Rollercoaster *The Unforgotten Coat* Frank Cottrell Boyce

Super-Readable Rollercoaster *Out of the Rubble* Sally Nicholls

Oxford Playscript *Anansi* Alistair Campbell

Chapter openers

How to use the chapter openers

The chapter openers include an introduction to the units with some questions to prompt students to think about the topic and to recall prior learning. The second part of the chapter opener is a learning overview that will show the route students will take through the chapter.

The chapter opener will help prepare students in understanding the texts covered in the units. It can be used to initiate a discussion about what students think might be covered in the chapter and to explore any background knowledge they have or might need to have. It can also be used to help students review their understanding at the end of the chapter and discuss what they have learned.

Encourage students to read the introduction individually or as a whole class. Discuss what texts they have already read that day, the last novel they might have read, instructions or signs on the way to school, etc.

These activities can be done individually or as a whole-class activity alongside a general discussion about the topic to help with any background knowledge students might need.

Key vocabulary: text, audience, purpose, form, narrative, non-narrative, fiction, non-fiction, prose, drama, poetry, dialect

Key vocabulary

The vocabulary introduced in the chapter opener forms the basis for the subsequent topics in the Student Book. These specialist items of terminology are building blocks for students to become familiar with and to begin to use with confidence in response to texts.

Students will have met much of this vocabulary during KS1 and KS2. However, some students may struggle to visualise the more abstract concepts. Visual reminders on classroom wall displays may help, as well as providing definitions to reinforce the meanings.

Metacognition

The chapter openers provide students with a broad range of stimuli to activate their prior knowledge and experience. The prompts are both visual and text-based, with images to engage students in the issues and themes relevant to the topic itself. Text boxes provide questions designed to engage students with thought-provoking ideas.

The activities in this chapter set out to make the implicit, explicit: to draw out what many students will already intuitively know but are not necessarily aware of knowing. The activities probe students' understanding and bring to the surface key ideas and concepts relating to written and spoken texts.

Make sure that students read about how to use these pages. Encourage students to review these pages before starting a new unit.

Use the statements in these boxes to review their learning when they finish a unit and to introduce the next unit.

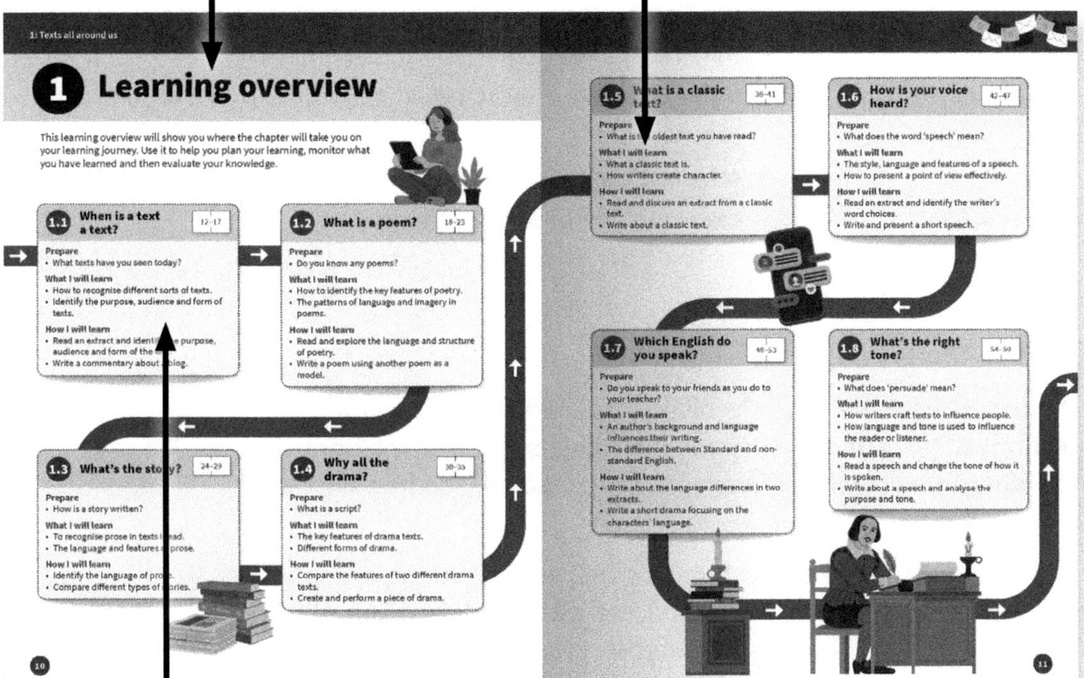
1: Texts all around us

1 Learning overview

This learning overview will show you where the chapter will take you on your learning journey. Use it to help you plan your learning, monitor what you have learned and then evaluate your knowledge.

1.1 When is a text a text? 12–17

Prepare
- What texts have you seen today?

What I will learn
- How to recognise different sorts of texts.
- Identify the purpose, audience and form of texts.

How I will learn
- Read an extract and identi[illegible]e purpose, audience and form of the [illegible]
- Write a commentary about [illegible] blog.

1.2 What is a poem? 18–23

Prepare
- Do you know any poems?

What I will learn
- How to identify the key features of poetry.
- The patterns of language and imagery in poems.

How I will learn
- Read and explore the language and structure of poetry.
- Write a poem using another poem as a model.

1.3 What's the sto[illegible]y? 24–29

Prepare
- How is a story written?

What I will learn
- To recognise prose in texts [illegible]ead.
- The language and features [illegible] prose.

How I will learn
- Identify the language of pro[illegible].
- Compare different types of [illegible]ories.

1.4 Why all the drama? 30–35

Prepare
- What is a script?

What I will learn
- The key features of drama texts.
- Different forms of drama.

How I will learn
- Compare the features of two different drama texts.
- Create and perform a piece of drama.

10

1.5 [illegible]at is a classic te[illegible]t? 36–41

Prepare
- What is t[illegible] oldest text you have read?

What I will learn
- What a classic text is.
- How writers create character.

How I will learn
- Read and discuss an extract from a classic text.
- Write about a classic text.

1.6 How is your voice heard? 42–47

Prepare
- What does the word 'speech' mean?

What I will learn
- The style, language and features of a speech.
- How to present a point of view effectively.

How I will learn
- Read an extract and identify the writer's word choices.
- Write and present a short speech.

1.7 Which English do you speak? 48–53

Prepare
- Do you speak to your friends as you do to your teacher?

What I will learn
- An author's background and language influences their writing.
- The difference between Standard and non-standard English.

How I will learn
- Write about the language differences in two extracts.
- Write a short drama focusing on the characters' language.

1.8 What's the right tone? 54–59

Prepare
- What does 'persuade' mean?

What I will learn
- How writers craft texts to influence people.
- How language and tone is used to influence the reader or listener.

How I will learn
- Read a speech and change the tone of how it is spoken.
- Write about a speech and analyse the purpose and tone.

11

The statements in these boxes will help prepare students for what they will be learning in each unit. Discuss them in order to prepare students for anything that they might find challenging.

1.1 When is a text a text?

Student Book pp 12–17

Unit focus

Objectives

Students will:

- learn to recognise different sorts of text
- understand how to identify the purpose, audience and form of a text
- write about a text, commenting on its key features.

Unit texts

- Captain Scott letter
- 'How not to care what other people think of you' Tavi Gevinson
- *A Lady's Life in the Rocky Mountains* Isabella Bird **WS**

Assessment

1.1 Mini-checkpoint quiz

Key terms

- **abstract noun** a noun that refers to an idea, quality or emotion, rather than a solid object, e.g. *happiness, truth, freedom*
- **audience** the people or person for whom a text is written or performed
- **compound word** a word that is made up of two or more other words. Some compound words have hyphens, but not all, e.g. *ear-splitting, suitcase, hedgehog*
- **fiction** a narrative that is imaginary or invented
- **form** the organisation of writing in a particular way, e.g. a letter or a poem
- **narrative** a story or account of connected events
- **non-fiction** real events or factual information
- **non-narrative** information that is not part of a sequence of events
- **purpose** the reason that a text is written
- **text** any form of written material

Introduction to the unit

Unit 1.1 *When is a text a text?* introduces students to the diversity of texts they encounter every day to demonstrate that not all texts that can be studied in English must come from old books. The unit questions what a text is, why different texts are created, and how we can identify who their intended audiences are.

Students are encouraged to consider texts in the broadest sense. Whether they are reading online messages, film subtitles, memes or the back of a cereal packet, they are still reading. All of those texts were written by someone, for an audience and a purpose, in a particular form, with its own conventions, and all of these aspects of reading and writing are a reason to study them.

Activities

Starter activity

Introduce the big idea of texts all around us by challenging students to find texts everywhere they go. Students can take photos of the texts they see and make a collage or a display according to purpose and audience or form. Students may initially characterise texts as books, possibly then suggesting plays, newspapers or magazines: traditional forms where stories or news are related. Ensure they understand the wider concept of a text before they begin Activity 1.

Activity 1

This activity will activate prior knowledge and develop self-awareness. Students may not appreciate how much they already understand about the texts they encounter daily. If appropriate, students could go on a textual treasure hunt around the school.

Activity 2 Building your knowledge

Encourage students to draw on their own experiences and knowledge to find texts as examples of each purpose. Students could work in small groups to create a display of texts organised according to purpose, for example, to instruct, to entertain, etc.

Activity 3 Building your knowledge

This activity provides students with the foundation for developing longer responses in later activities. The table allows students to show what they understand about the *who*, *where*, *what* and *why* of a range of texts. Ask students to add their own ideas to the table.

Stretch yourself

The stretch activity challenges students to consider how having an audience of a single person might affect the writer of a text, in contrast to an audience of many; or an audience that is familiar rather than strangers. This has particular resonance with young people who are likely to encounter social media and helps them to navigate an online environment where texts can quickly move from a private audience to a global public one.

Kerboodle

The following activities can be replaced by the text and activities on 1.1 *A Lady's Life in the Rocky Mountains* worksheet.

Activity 4 Building your knowledge

This activity explores Scott's letter, with open-ended questions to encourage longer, more detailed responses. Some students could be supported by offering a range of options if appropriate, for example, *Do you think Captain Scott felt angry/sad/hopeful/desperate/lonely/anxious/disappointed?*

Activity 5 Building your knowledge

Students are provided with an opportunity to use their writing skills to demonstrate their understanding of the key concepts, drawing on their own experiences as the basis for the letter-writing. Students may need further prompts to consider events in their own lives which might form the basis of their letter. This activity could be used to teach a specific metacognitive strategy. Use the list of what to include to generate a list of success criteria, such as 'I know that the structure of a letter includes a date, a greeting and a signature'. These criteria could be referred to when students are writing to check if they have included the features of a letter, and then referred to when reviewing their finished piece of writing.

Activity 6 Boosting your vocabulary

As the blog contains some Americanisms, it gives an opportunity for a discussion to explore the differences between British and American English.

In part b, the abstract nouns 'shame' and 'guilt' provide opportunities for further work on this important word class. Students need to be familiar with the words and their meanings, understand the concept of their abstract nature, and then begin to use them in response to the texts they read and in their own creative and rhetorical writing. In part c, some students might need more support to think of words they can put together to create a compound word and will need suggestions or to write sentences using the suggestions in the key terms box.

Activity 7 Putting it all together

This activity builds on the skills and knowledge introduced earlier in the unit. This allows stronger students to demonstrate an extended understanding, but also provides support with a student example as a model. Encourage students to refer to the Building your knowledge section after they have answered parts a to c to check whether their answers are correct.

Activity 8 Putting it all together

This activity encourages students to engage with the writer's perspective as a concept. It prepares students for later units that focus on the writer's perspective and where students develop their understanding of how those perspectives are conveyed. It could be done as a whole-class activity or as a group. The latter would lend itself to an opportunity to observe students and identify any misconceptions that they have on what a point of view is and what a writer's purpose might be. Finish the unit by asking students to reflect on whether their learning in this unit will help them with the next units.

Additional activities

Ask students to collect and bring into school images of texts they have encountered in their local and home environments. Depending on the school's policy on the use of mobile phones, this functionality can be exploited to good effect in exploring online texts, with the benefit that it validates students' experience of the Internet.

1.2 What is a poem?

Student Book pp 18–23

Unit focus

Objectives

Students will:

- learn about some of the key features of poetry
- discover patterns of language and imagery in poems
- write a poem, building on a modelled structure.

Unit texts

- 'I Want a Poem' Shukria Rezaei
- 'The Factory' Letitia Elizabeth Landon
- 'Advice to a Teenage Daughter' Isobel Thrilling **WS**

Assessment

1.2 Mini-checkpoint quiz

Key terms

- **drama** a play written for performance on stage or to be listened to
- **metaphor** a comparison that says one thing *is* something else, e.g. *Amy was a rock*
- **poetry** a piece of writing often arranged in short lines and stanzas, following a pattern of sounds, and expressing feelings and ideas with great imagination
- **prose** written language in its ordinary form, rather than poetry or drama
- **repetition** using the same word or phrase more than once
- **rhyme** using the same sound to end words, particularly at the ends of lines
- **rhythm** the pattern of beats in a line of music or poetry
- **simile** a comparison of one thing to another, using *as* or *like*, e.g. *He swam like a fish*
- **stanza** a group of lines in a poem with a line space before and after it

Introduction to the unit

Unit 1.2 *What is a poem?* encourages students to explore the wider boundaries of what we consider to be poetry. The unit invites students to consider the common features of different types of poems and the wide range of texts that can be classed as poetry. The unit explores what makes poems unique as texts, how the language of poems can create powerful effects, and how to develop a personal response to poetry. The activities build towards the task of writing a poem in which students can demonstrate their understanding of how to shape words and images within the conventions of a given poetic structure.

Activities

Starter activity

Students will have met a number of poems at KS2 and could be encouraged to bring in their favourite poems, or identify their favourite imagery from these. Students are likely to be more familiar with poetry in the form of song lyrics, which can provide exciting and valuable material for study, while reinforcing one of the principles of this topic – that texts are all around us, that they are relevant to our everyday lives and that texts matter. Regarding the possibility of contentious lyrics, parameters can be set to help control any such issues.

Activity 1

The simple questions activate students' prior knowledge and experience of poetry and song lyrics, and encourage students to appreciate the similarities and differences between poetry and song lyrics. Students could be asked what they think about poetry, whether their attitude will impact their learning, and, if negative, how they can overcome that attitude.

Kerboodle

The following activities can be replaced by the text and activities on 1.2 'Advice to a Teenage Daughter' worksheet.

Activity 2

Students have an opportunity to explore what they know about imagery, sensory language, mood and patterns of words. Teachers can use this activity to identify students with limited prior knowledge of these word classes and can focus their interventions accordingly. Exploring the language of the poem might help those students struggling with this activity, for example, ask students to check what a colander is and think about the pattern it would make when pressed into pastry.

Activity 3 Boosting your vocabulary

The powerful words selected from the poem in each part of this activity will enrich students' own writing and speaking. The contrast drawn between 'rich', 'gleam' and 'stings' could be extended to other surprising contrasts, for example to fruit, such as a kiwi, which is dull and hairy. If possible, show students a real prism to enhance their understanding and interest.

Activity 4 Building your knowledge

Students could discuss part a of the activity as a whole class or in groups to then feed back to the rest of the class. Some students may need support with part b in understanding that the poem is being compared to saffron, so they will need support to consider what a poem and saffron might have in common, for example review the word 'vibrant'. Students are invited to create similes of their own. This can be extended to many different topics. Discourage students from relying on over-used similes such as 'cool as a cucumber'. Suggesting a focus such as the sea, the wind, a jungle, etc. may stimulate students' creative energy.

Activity 5 Building your knowledge

This activity would work well as a group activity. Before they discuss each of the questions, make sure that students know what is meant by the structure of a poem, e.g. how it is written; that the language used/particular words help to create images and moods, e.g. the use of 'shade', 'dark', 'tempest', 'shadow', 'despair', 'shuts out', 'appalling cry', 'resigned', 'sicken' and 'die'; and remind students what 'audience' and 'purpose' mean.

Stretch yourself

The open-ended stretch activity encourages students to develop a slightly longer response, considering how the poet conveys her message so powerfully. Students could focus on the ideas in the poem, explaining more about the Victorian context and placing the poem within a period of history when social reformers were working to improve children's welfare. Alternatively, they could be encouraged to link the use of imagery and word choice to the ideas and explain how the images offer a powerful criticism of the treatment of children.

Activity 6 Putting it all together

The final task is to write a poem following specific steps. Some students may find using Rezaei's poem structure as a model helpful. Teachers could also show how to write the first stanza by modelling writing and explaining the choice of language and structure being used. It is worth reminding students that Rezaei keeps the imagery in her poem consistent, by relating each comparison to food and celebration which establishes and maintains a specific mood of joy and feasting. If students try to mix images of confetti and cobwebs, for example, they will not establish a consistent mood, which is what they should aim to do in this activity. For example, they could link cobwebs and crows' feathers or confetti and candyfloss, but should not mix the two. The poems can be collated in a class compilation and even published on the school website. Students could be asked to reflect on their learning and if their opinion of poetry has changed and how they were able to overcome any challenges about reading poetry.

Additional activities

Some students may benefit from additional support in understanding the concept of associative thinking involved in similes and other figurative language. A Venn diagram which sets out the features of the two things being compared can be a useful way to encourage students to appreciate visually what they have in common. Reading poems aloud is a very useful way to establish understanding of the abstract concepts of rhyme and rhythm and to encourage an appreciation of the similarities between poetry and song.

1.3 What's the story?

Student Book pp 24–29

Unit focus

Objectives

Students will:

- learn to recognise prose and understand its different forms
- explore some of the language and features used in prose
- compare different types of stories written in prose.

Unit texts

- Amazon rainforest article
- *Pigeon English* Stephen Kelman
- 'Five young entrepreneurs' Sarah LeBrecque **WS**
- *Diary of a Wimpy Kid* Jeff Kinney **WS**

Assessment

1.3 Mini-checkpoint quiz

Key terms

- **adjective** a word that describes a noun
- **adverb** a word that you use with a verb, adjective or other adverb that tells you how, when or where something happened
- **first-person narrative** a story told by someone as if they were involved in the events themselves, using first-person pronouns, e.g. *I* and *we*
- **infer** to work something out from what is seen, said or done, even though it is not stated directly
- **narrator** a person who tells a story, especially in a book, play or film
- **quotation** a word or phrase from a text
- **third-person narrative** a story told by someone who was not involved in the events themselves, using third-person pronouns, e.g. *he, she, they*

Introduction to the unit

Unit 1.3 *What's the story?* explores the ways in which stories are told, and encourages students to appreciate the breadth and diversity of stories in our lives. It contrasts fictional stories, characters and settings, with factual texts about real people and real events. The unit encourages students to recognise and understand the differences between these narrative genres, and also to see the features they have in common. It introduces the concept of narrative writing and how perspective is shaped by the writer.

Activities

Starter activity

There are likely to be many examples of prose texts in the classroom, especially fiction. It would be useful to add a variety of non-fiction prose texts: travel writing, autobiographies, biographies, how-to guides, as well as newspapers and magazines. Displays of these will remind students of the breadth and diversity of prose texts. As the unit progresses, these prose texts can be categorised and re-categorised as narrative or non-narrative; first or third person; chronological or non-chronological.

Activity 1

Students could be encouraged to look at the previous text extracts that they have encountered to find other types of texts and to consider how prose and poetry are different. Look back at the poem 'The Factory' in Unit 1.2 and ask students to consider if the poem has more impact on the reader than a prose text would. Ask questions such as: *Does the imagery in the poem make the setting worse?*

Kerboodle

The following activities can be replaced by the text and activities on 1.3 'Five young entrepreneurs' worksheet.

Activity 2

The terms introduced in Unit 1.1 are reinforced in the questions in this activity, and students are encouraged to apply their knowledge to the text extract. Students could be asked about what strategies they used to find the answers to the questions. If necessary, ask more specific questions about the clues that indicate the text type, e.g. point to the headline and ask where students have seen something like that before.

Activity 3 Boosting your vocabulary

Ask students what they remember about adverbs and adjectives from KS2. This is a chance to identify any students whose understanding of word classes is not secure.

As an additional activity, the words 'dehydration' and 'malnutrition' could be highlighted within the text. Ask students to work out the root word and then the prefix – a term that they should know from KS2. Discuss the prefixes 'mal' and 'de' and how they modify the meaning. Students could be asked to make a list of other words with 'mal' and 'de' prefixes and explain how they change the meaning. Students may need help recognising that sometimes 'mal' (still meaning 'bad') is a stem, not a prefix, such as 'malice', 'malevolent'; and that 'mal' and 'de' at the start of words are not always prefixes, e.g. 'mallard', 'male', 'desperate' and 'decent'.

Activity 4 Building your knowledge

Draw students' attention to the Tip box, which reminds students that there can be more than one purpose. Emphasise that there is no single right answer to the question, as the purpose could be to advise, to inform, to explain, to celebrate, for example.

Activity 5 Building your knowledge

Students are tasked with finding evidence of whether the text is fiction or non-fiction. If necessary, offer support by identifying relevant features: use of dates; names; statistics; factual language; non-chronological structure with the final event being told first.

Activity 6 Building your knowledge

Before students consider the text in the Student Book, they could discuss what they already know about first and third-person narratives to activate prior knowledge. Considering using the opposite type of narrative can be a useful way of exploring what effect each has on the reliability and excitement of the prose text. To help students who may struggle, show them the differences between first, second and third person in an example text.

Activity 7 Building your knowledge

This activity encourages an inferential understanding of the *Pigeon English* extract. The explanation above the activity demonstrates how students can structure their response and is a foundation for the longer responses required at KS3 and KS4. A prior discussion on students' knowledge of inference from their learning at KS2 may be useful. Check that students understand the vocabulary and punctuation in the quotations.

Stretch yourself

This activity is an opportunity for students to write a more synoptic response to a broader task, explaining what they infer from the extract about the character of the narrator. Encourage students to support their points with short, relevant quotations. Their inferences may vary according to their interpretation but all are acceptable provided they are supported by the text.

Activity 8 Building your knowledge

This activity revisits similes. Students could remind themselves of the comparative images they created in Unit 1.2. The focus here is to explain about the effect of similes, making explicit their knowledge and explaining the mechanics of a simile analytically.

Activity 9 Putting it all together

The final task draws together the knowledge students have gained over the previous units. The chart allows students to demonstrate their understanding without constructing a longer written response. In part b students explain their understanding. The connectives suggested will support students in structuring their answers, providing the linguistic bridge between their comments on the two texts.

Additional activities

Exploring a wider range of texts can help students grasp abstract concepts such as fact and fiction, chronological and non-chronological, narrative and non-narrative. It is easier to see the pattern among many examples than among only two or three.

1.4 Why all the drama?

Student Book pp 30–35

Unit focus

Objectives

Students will:

- learn to identify the key features of drama texts
- explore and compare two forms of drama
- create, perform and record their own piece of drama.

Unit texts

- 🔈 *Romeo and Juliet* William Shakespeare
- 🔈 'Here Be Dragons' Jordan Cobb
- Ⓚ 'Aladdin and the Wonderful Lamp' Neville Teller **WS**

Assessment

Ⓚ 1.4 Mini-checkpoint quiz; Chapter 1 Checkpoint 1 reading assessment; Chapter 1 Checkpoint 1 writing assessment

Key terms

- **character** a person in a drama or story
- **climax** when the action is at its most exciting or interesting
- **conflict** a struggle or disagreement between people
- **dialogue** words spoken by characters
- **monologue** a speech by one character
- **setting** where the action takes place

Introduction to the unit

Unit 1.4 *Why all the drama?* illustrates the breadth and diversity of drama texts in the same way that the two previous units have exemplified the range and variety of prose and poetry. Drama can take many forms. Although stage plays in performance at theatres may be beyond the daily experience of many young people, drama has become far more accessible over time. Firstly radio, closely followed by film and television, are obvious examples of how new technology and new platforms have met the needs of a wider audience and created an ever-increasing appetite for drama. The Internet has brought an explosion of new ways to broadcast and consume drama content, including drama on demand. This unit explores the common features of drama texts and recognises their differences, too.

Activities

Starter activity

This unit offers opportunities for an exploration of multimedia texts alongside more traditional written texts, validating the experiences of many students whose on-screen viewing is likely to contribute significantly to their cultural lives. Some adults may be inclined to dismiss this experience as lacking cultural or educational value, but what's important is to ensure that students can become critical viewers of on-screen content, making informed judgements about what is valuable and what is not.

Allowing students to present a clip of their favourite online, film or TV drama to the class, with a brief explanation of what they think makes it 'good', is a way to get students talking about the features of drama as well as introduce ideas of quality.

Activity 1

This activity introduces students to the concept of drama as a literary form and challenges them to consider the breadth of platforms where drama is broadcast and can be viewed. Students are likely to be familiar with watching television, watching drama on a phone or iPad, watching YouTube video and listening to podcasts on their phones. This is a good opportunity to define drama as distinct from content which is dramatic. A show like *I'm a Celebrity ... Get Me Out of Here!* may appear to be a drama, but it is a documentary as the people are real and not characters, whereas *Horrible Histories* is a drama although the action is based on real events.

Kerboodle
The following activities can be replaced by the text and activities on 1.4 'Aladdin and the Wonderful Lamp' worksheet.

Activity 2 Boosting your vocabulary
To ensure students are not overwhelmed by Shakespeare's unfamiliar vocabulary, words have been selected from the extract and explained. This will give students confidence to engage with what they may perceive as a 'difficult' text.

Activity 3
This task is a challenging one but can be modified to make it more accessible. Students could be given a finite number of lines of dialogue to write (ten, for example) and encouraged to create a conversation between two characters. The characters could be defined as a parent and child, for example, and even the topic could be provided, e.g. an argument about eating breakfast or staying out late. Modelling how to write the start of a dialogue and asking students to create their own, or to continue the modelling, will help students practise writing drama and setting it out as a dialogue rather than prose. More confident students will enjoy the challenge of the task unsupported, creating dialogue on a similar theme to the extract from *Romeo and Juliet*. Encourage them to stop after writing a few lines to check their writing against the modelled text or the extract in the Student Book to make sure that they have continued to write dialogue and not switched to prose.

Activity 4 Building your knowledge
This reading task develops skills needed throughout KS3 and KS4. Building on the focus on inference in Unit 1.3, students find quotations from the extract that evidence the given inferences about characters, using skills such as retrieval and inferential understanding. In part b, the examples are valuable models on how to structure their responses. In part a, the quotations could be provided for students to match with the given character traits.

Activity 5 Building your knowledge
Discuss the extract with students and consider the themes. Students might be supported further by offering them some choices: young love, forbidden love, family relationships, friends and enemies, social hierarchies, family problems, secrets.

Activity 6 Building your knowledge
Students can demonstrate their understanding of drama features in a graphic presentation, either individually, or in groups. They could include images or drawings to represent the different aspects of drama texts. This is an opportunity for teachers to assess their knowledge and identify students who may need more support in the next activity.

Activity 7 Putting it all together
This writing task invites students to create and perform an audio drama. The task provides support, encouraging students to work through several steps, considering characters, setting, action and dialogue. Students should also establish the purpose and audience of their writing to apply their knowledge from the previous units. Setting a time limit or a length of script will help students to focus their ideas. A five-minute drama is a reasonable expectation and restricting the number of characters to four is a helpful limit. For further support, a theme or topic could be provided.

Performance and recording of these dramas will follow a period of rehearsal. The dramas could be adapted for live performance, possibly involving cross-curricular links with the Drama department in school.

Additional activities
Modern-language versions of Shakespeare might prove useful (though they can be uninspiring in terms of their unpoetic language) to help students understand the plot of the story and a 'way into' the language of Shakespeare. Alternative ways of making Shakespeare accessible would be seeing *Romeo and Juliet* in performance, or watching a film extract. As in previous units, exposure to a wider range of examples of the dramatic form can help students to understand the common features more easily.

1.5 What is a classic text?

Student Book pp 36–41

Unit focus

Objectives

Students will:

- learn what qualities make a text a classic
- explore how language and structural features are used to help to build character
- write about a classic text, showing their understanding of its appeal.

Unit texts

- *The Lion, the Witch and the Wardrobe* C.S. Lewis
- *Alice's Adventures in Wonderland* Lewis Carroll **WS**

Assessment

1.5 Mini-checkpoint quiz

Key terms

- **fantasy** an imaginary story that is not based on reality
- **genre** a type of story, e.g. *horror, romance, adventure, science fiction*
- **modal verb** a verb that works with another verb to show that something needs to happen or might possibly happen, e.g. *must, shall, will, should, would, can, could, may* and *might*
- **mythical** from a myth, a traditional story that often includes supernatural beings
- **structural feature** a feature used by a writer to give a text its overall shape

Introduction to the unit

Unit 1.5 *What is a classic text?* introduces students to classic literature in an accessible way. Rather than overwhelm students with a barrage of traditional, historical literature, this unit takes a 20th-century children's classic text as the basis for exploring the qualities often found in classic texts. It might be helpful to reference any film or television adaptations to engage students, and help them to draw on prior knowledge of plotlines. The unit demonstrates why some texts endure and prepares students to consider the influence of contemporary writers and speakers.

Activities

Starter activity

It is useful to consider a range of classic texts, aimed at adults as well as younger readers. Many students will be able to draw on their experience at KS2 where they may have encountered classic texts. Start by eliciting students' preconceptions about writers such as Shakespeare and Dickens, perhaps by thinking about film or television adaptations that students might have some knowledge of.

Once students are secure in understanding what classic texts are, ask questions about who they think decides about what makes a classic text.

Traditionally, the status of an author had an influence and historically white men were considered to have a higher status than anyone else. These authors had more access to education and, therefore, were more privileged to write and be published. Encourage students to challenge this view, by asking what has changed in society and why there is a need to include a broader range of authors and voices in what is considered a classic text. Discuss how the messages and language used in classic texts can be problematic, as society has changed since they were written and the impact they have has also changed.

Activity 1

Before starting the activity, revisit the learning from the previous units and discuss the purpose, audience and form of the extract.

Activity 1 encourages students to consider what they know about classic texts. Broaden the scope of what constitutes a classic text, incorporating fairy tales, folk tales, myths and legends, as well as traditional writers such as Shakespeare and Dickens. Students could consider texts such as *Harry Potter* and question why it might become a classic or not. Ask students to think about the promotional power of film and the Internet, which previously were not available to historical writers of literary texts.

Kerboodle

The following activities can be replaced by the text and activities on 1.5 *Alice's Adventures in Wonderland* worksheet.

Activity 2 Boosting your vocabulary

This activity expands students' familiarity with a range of more sophisticated words: 'inquisitive', 'melancholy' and 'reign'. It also explores the use of modal verbs, which some students may recall from KS2 while others may need to review them. It might be beneficial to pre-teach these, or ask students to do this activity in groups to support each other's understanding. The use of modal verbs is particularly important for the development of students' ability to express a perspective.

Activity 3 Building your knowledge

In this activity, students are invited to engage with several elements common to many classic texts. The intention is to explore the breadth and diversity of these timeless ideas as well as the recurrence across time and across different cultures and media. The broader the range of examples students consider, the better they will appreciate the concept of timeless themes and narrative structures. The activity could be carried out individually, in pairs, in small groups or as a whole-class discussion. Students could make notes of their discussions and feed back their ideas and examples to the rest of the class.

Activities 4 and 5 Building your knowledge

These activities are designed to support students in developing a disciplinary approach to writing about texts. They encourage students to appreciate how the features that writers use can build character, and how students can use textual references to support their understanding of how this works. Activity 4 focuses on features and their effects on the characters, providing a scaffold for matching them. Activity 5 offers more independence for students to select their own textual details from the extract. Students are supported through the process of commenting on writers' methods which lays the foundation for many of the skills they will need to demonstrate throughout KS3 and KS4.

Activity 6 Putting it all together

Having completed the preparation work in the previous activities, students are asked to develop a longer, synoptic response to a reading question. The annotations are designed to help students see the different elements coming together, and support them in writing their own response to the other three features from Activity 4. If some students find the mechanical approach restrictive, they should be encouraged to add further detail to any of the different elements, using the framework as a launch pad. Some students will benefit from the very structured, stepped approach: introduction, feature, example/quotation, effect, explanation linked to the question. Students could write each of these separately before combining them into a paragraph. Alternatively, model an answer explicitly, using the structure in the Student Book, talking through the thought process in answering the question.

Additional activities

To stretch students, ask them to read the whole of *The Lion, the Witch and the Wardrobe*, as well as the rest of the Narnia series. Students might also like to draw on their own imagination in writing about an encounter between a child and a fantasy character or mythical creature. Texts such as *Alice's Adventures in Wonderland* by Lewis Carroll and *Coraline* by Neil Gaiman are interesting models to explore. Watching the film of *The Lion, the Witch and the Wardrobe* may help some students to orientate themselves around the text extract, and help them to appreciate the fantasy genre, and identify more of the features of classic texts.

1.6 How is your voice heard?

Student Book pp 42–47

Unit focus

Objectives

Students will:

- learn how to share their views effectively
- explore the context, style and features of a powerful speech
- write and present a short speech to express their point of view.

Unit texts

- 'The Danger of a Single Story' TED Talk Chimamanda Ngozi Adichie
- Kit de Waal's speech on diversity **WS**

Assessment

1.6 Mini-checkpoint quiz

Key terms

- **anecdote** a short or entertaining story about real people or events
- **antonym** a word that has the opposite meaning of a particular word
- **context** the time, place and influences on a text from when it was written, and from when it is read, which shape our understanding of the text
- **tone** the writer's feeling or attitude expressed towards their subject
- **transcript** a written record of spoken words

Introduction to the unit

Unit 1.6 *How is your voice heard?* builds on the previous unit's focus on timeless voices and how students can begin to think about getting their own voices heard by writing and speaking for themselves. Now, more than ever, the Internet has created a democracy where a global audience is free and easy for many people to access. There is an explosion in the self-publishing of stories and texts online, with many platforms providing opportunities for people of all ages to speak out on whatever subject they choose. Media education is an imperative for students growing up in a world dominated by media texts.

Activities

Starter activity

To engage and begin a discussion with students about the spoken language and performance elements of this unit, it is helpful to start with the sort of content students are familiar with. Platforms such as TikTok and YouTube have almost infinite material and students will enjoy demonstrating their expertise to teachers. Video on topics ranging from puppies to paddle-boarding provide the springboard for students to view this content not as a consumer, but as a questioning critic. Students can progress from these largely informal spoken-language texts, to watching more formal documentaries. This should provoke a discussion of formal/informal language; specialist/non-specialist vocabulary; audience, purpose, form and impact or influence.

Activity 1

This activity directly activates prior knowledge for this activity. The questions encourage students to draw on their broader understanding and experience of the spoken word around them and consider how it compares with their experience of the written texts around them. It is better to share video as a whole class and control the content rather than risk students working in pairs or small groups.

Kerboodle

The following activities can be replaced by the text and activities on 1.6 Kit de Waal's speech on diversity worksheet.

Activity 2 Boosting your vocabulary

Part a looks at the word 'campus' and asks questions to help students to work out its meaning. This would be an effective whole-class activity, asking students to discuss the questions in pairs before giving an answer. In part b, students are introduced to the Frayer model which explores the connotations and origins of words. Ask students to create a Frayer model for the word 'vulnerable', based on the example in the Student Book.

Activity 3 Building your knowledge

This activity encourages students to reflect on the context of texts. Some students will understand the abstract idea of context without difficulty; others will need support. Discuss how everything that surrounds a text can be considered context and is relevant to how a text is understood. Important factors such as ethnicity and gender will have an impact on both the reader and the writer. This central aspect of context provides a foundation on which later discussions can build.

Stretch yourself

The stretch activity invites students to consider how their own response to texts is influenced by their personal context. A student's gender, ethnicity, age and wider circumstances, as well as their experience as a reader and writer, will all have an impact on their response. They could present their views in a blog or vlog, using anecdotes to illustrate their perspective.

Activity 4 Building your knowledge

This activity covers a range of knowledge, where students are encouraged to consider the tone of the speech and describe it using adjectives. For part b, students could work in pairs to read a paragraph of the speech aloud. This is effective in encouraging less confident students to practise speaking aloud. Each student could challenge their partner to read the speech using a particular tone. This will be a good opportunity to observe students and to identify those who find speaking out loud a challenge, as well as those students who are less fluent in their reading.

Activities 5 and 6 Building your knowledge

Activities 5 and 6 are linked, with a discussion of statements followed by expressing a personal opinion. The statements are deliberately provocative to encourage students to develop a response. However, sensitivity will be required and discussions will vary depending on the demographic of the class. Collaborative speaking skills are required, and students should be reminded to take turns, listen attentively and ask questions to elicit more detail. In Activity 6 students are expected to explain why they changed the statements in Activity 5. They could work in pairs or in small groups if some students feel less confident in presenting to the rest of the class. The bulleted guidance could be used as success criteria for how they orally presented their view. Perhaps ask pairs to discuss the points after listening to their partner's performance.

Activity 7 and 8 Putting it all together

Activity 7 offers a step-by-step guide to writing a perspective on a topic of the student's choice. Providing a choice of topics will support those who cannot think of something independently, without dictating a topic which doesn't interest them at all. The stepped approach provides a structure for students constructing an argument. The activity also provides a model for students to draw on for inspiration and guidance. Activity 8 is the presentation of the speech to a whole-class audience or a student partner, depending on the confidence of students involved. This may be challenging for many students and if they struggle to perform their speech to an audience, they could record or film it instead.

Additional activities

Encourage students to listen to more TED Talks at home, such as William Kamkwamba, or even TED Talks by children, such as Miranda Wang and Jeanny Yao and Richard Turere. Ask students to find out other ways that they can listen to speeches or talks, such as on YouTube. They could be encouraged to compare speeches by famous people in history to speeches that have been made in more modern times and to discuss what the differences are in tone and presentation.

1.7 Which English do you speak?

Student Book pp 48–53

Unit focus

Objectives

Students will:

- learn how texts are influenced by a writer's background and the language they use
- explore differences between Standard and non-standard English
- write a drama script, including characters who are code-switching.

Unit texts

- 'Running' Benjamin Zephaniah
- OBE article Benjamin Zephaniah
- 'Search for My Tongue' Sujata Bhatt **WS**

Assessment

1.7 Mini-checkpoint quiz

Key terms

- **bilingual** able to speak two languages
- **code-switching** moving between different levels of formality in language, e.g. between Standard English and non-standard English
- **dialect** a form of a language linked to a specific region, e.g. Geordie in Newcastle upon Tyne
- **non-standard English** an informal version of English, often used with family and friends, including slang and regional variations
- **root** the core of a word that has meaning. It may or may not be a complete word
- **Standard English** a widely recognised formal version of English, not linked to any region, but used in schools, exams, official publications and in public announcements
- **suffix** a word or group of letters placed at the end of another word or root to add to or change its meaning

Introduction to the unit

Unit 1.7 *Which English do you speak?* invites students to think about the language they use to express themselves. The unit explores issues of Standard and non-standard English and the use of dialect, and touches on the experience of being bilingual. Data suggests that significant numbers of British students are bilingual; many speak a regional or other dialect; and almost all will use non-standard English daily. In an increasingly global, multilingual world, this unit helps students to recognise the diversity of language and prepares them for the complex demands on their language skills.

Activities

Starter activity

It might be useful to start by exploring the variety of languages spoken among students within the class, or among students and staff in the school. This could take the form of a survey of the whole school community. With students writing questions that could be sensitive, this will need adult guidance to appropriately elicit the required information. Students could carry out the survey at lunchtime, for example. A similar survey could be carried out among family members for homework.

Activity 1

This activity explores students' prior knowledge and helps them to make explicit what they know implicitly about language use and identity. The questions prompt an appreciation of students' own diverse language experiences. This could be a paired activity to develop collaborative oracy skills, with an opportunity to develop confidence in speaking in front of others when students feed back to the class.

Kerboodle

The following activities can be replaced by the text and activities on 1.7 'Search for My Tongue' worksheet.

Activity 2 Boosting your vocabulary

Before they begin the activity, students can be encouraged to draw on prior knowledge from KS2 of root words and suffixes. Words can be collected in lists and word families developed and displayed on classroom walls. Use this activity to observe students' understanding of root words and identify students who might need extra support with their spelling knowledge. The activity will also lend itself to discussion prompts about the etymology of words.

Activity 3

This activity starts with a structured comparison of the features of two text extracts. The table helps to structure the comparison, with categories such as form, language, audience and purpose, directing the focus of students. The follow-up questions encourage a more analytical response, encouraging students to think carefully about why the writer has made those choices. These questions could be answered in pairs or small groups, with a chairperson nominated to feed back the group's response to the rest of the class.

Activity 4

In this activity, students consider their own use of language and dialect or non-standard features. The glossary of dialect words could be written as a digital resource and posted on the school's website as an example of work completed in English lessons. It could prompt a wider project exploring language use in the local area, involving surveys and questionnaires for older people in the community, collating a much larger glossary of local language use.

Stretch yourself

Discuss various ideas, such as how Standard English has been used by royalty, politicians and people in authority and how this might have had an influence.

Activity 5 Building your knowledge

This activity compares two language versions of the same school report. Some students might benefit from a limit such as finding five differences.

Activity 6 Building your knowledge

The statements in this activity form the foundation for a discussion of language and identity. They are phrased to provoke a strong response from students. Then, in pairs or small groups, students discuss the statements, establishing a personal perspective on each. Using the questions *Why?* and *How?*, and re-introducing the idea of context should encourage students to develop a more detailed and substantial response and helps students to think about how circumstances affect the language we use.

Activity 7 Putting it all together

Students should refer to Unit 1.4 to remind themselves of the features of drama. Students could work in groups, improvising a variety of scenes, developing a range of characters and language styles and registers, and considering a narrative arc: introduction, rising action, climax, falling action and resolution. Remind students about the characters' use of language and how they may code-switch when the teacher arrives on the scene, or how they might not if they are trying to keep their conversation secret, or if they make the teacher code-switch to show that they want to impress the student characters.

Stretch yourself

Students could work in groups to annotate their dramas to show why and when the language changes.

Additional activities

Students will benefit in terms of confidence from the oral-based work in this unit, and from experiencing validation through the focus on their own use of language. Students could be encouraged to find and read more poems by Benjamin Zephaniah or by other poets, such as George the Poet and Amanda Graham.

1.8 What's the right tone?

Student Book pp 54–59

Unit focus

Objectives

Students will:

- learn how writers craft texts to persuade others to their viewpoint
- explore how writers use language and tone to influence their audience
- comment on the effect of language choices and tone in a speech.

Unit texts

- Transcript of Malala Yousafzai's speech to the UN, 2013
- Extract from Air Ambulance charity website
- Marcus Rashford's letter to the government **WS**
- 'How to get a puppy or dog responsibly' Dogs Trust **WS**

Assessment

1.8 Mini-checkpoint quiz; Chapter 1 Checkpoint 2 speaking and listening assessment; Chapter 1 Checkpoint 2 reading assessment

Key terms

contrast to compare to show a difference

tricolon a pattern of three words or phrases grouped together to be memorable and have impact

Introduction to the unit

Unit 1.8 *What's the right tone?* draws on the previous units, with a focus on the writer's use of language and tone in texts which influence readers and audiences. Students are encouraged to engage with spoken and written texts, as a link to a video of the speech is included. The unit outcomes are based on being able to develop a written response to the methods used in the text.

The unit deals with the subject of terrorism and the Taliban. The activities will need to be implemented sensitively, especially if students have differing cultural backgrounds, and also because of the recent events in Afghanistan with the Taliban taking control of the country.

Activities

Starter activity

Students could find out more about Malala Yousafzai and the fact that she began her writing career before she became famous after the terrorist attack. She was invited to write a blog for the BBC website on her experiences as a schoolgirl in an area controlled by the Taliban. Students could read contemporary news reports about the attack on Malala to provide a context for the speech. This reinforces the concept of context influencing both the writing and reading of texts, as Malala's recovery and success influence the impact of past events on readers now, compared with the reaction of readers in 2012.

Activity 1

This activity encourages a reflective approach to the influence of those around us who speak to persuade us of their viewpoint. This could include influencers on YouTube, for example, who often have a commercial purpose or financial gain in making video. It is interesting to invite students to be critical of these influencers and explore what their purpose is in trying to influence viewers.

Kerboodle

The following activities can be replaced by the text and activities on 1.8 Marcus Rashford's letter to government worksheet.

Activity 2 Boosting your vocabulary

This activity encompasses a range of approaches to broaden vocabulary use. One of these which may resonate with students is the difference between the words 'activist' and 'terrorist'. It would be inappropriate to ignore these words, despite their sensitivity, and Malala Yousafzai uses them openly and explicitly in her speech. Exploring the connotations of these words is an opportunity to remind students of the seriousness of some words and their power in influencing readers and audiences. For these reasons, the words should not be used lightly. Any discussion will need strict moderation.

Activity 3

This activity reinforces the learning about audience and purpose in Units 1.1 to 1.4 by inviting students to write a paragraph about the different purposes and audience of the speech. It may be helpful to work through the speech as a whole class, one paragraph at a time, to identify where and how the writer's purpose changes.

Activity 4 Building your knowledge

This activity invites students to look at how tone is created using particular vocabulary and phrasing. The selection of words that establish the tone of the speech is valuable as it encourages a detailed reading of the transcript. Students should be encouraged to consider the connotations of the language chosen, exploring the effects of individual words and phrases. It can be useful to provide students with alternative vocabulary to support their understanding of why one word has a different impact from another. For example, the phrase 'They thought that the bullet would silence us' would have a different impact if it said 'they thought that their actions would stop us.'

Activity 5 Building your knowledge

In this activity there are opportunities to read aloud followed by questions related to the tone and impact of the words. Writing a personal response might reinforce the element of self-reflection and careful thought. Other students may benefit from this as a small-group speaking activity.

Activity 6 Building your knowledge

The examples in this activity provide the basis for further discussion of tone and its role in influencing readers. The model provided in the Student Book supports students in developing their own reading analysis of the second example, as well as supporting their vocabulary knowledge. It might be useful to read through this example and discuss the language as a class. Part c could be modelled for students who might need more support. Students should understand the thought process of identifying the feelings of the second writer and then how to write a paragraph explaining the tone.

Activity 7 Putting it all together

This activity challenges students to demonstrate their understanding of audience, purpose and tone, which they have explored throughout the preceding units. Students should work through the question parts. If appropriate, support students by supplying them with suitable quotations from the extract, such as 'Can you imagine how terrified she must have been?' A guide of a paragraph per question part might be helpful for students or, if students need more oracy opportunities, they could be asked to orally respond to each part or work in a group of three, each taking one part.

Additional activities

Tone is, by nature, abstract and in a written text it can often be difficult to pinpoint and comment on. In a spoken text, the speaker's tone can be easier to identify, even if finding evidence to support it can be difficult. Watching lots of spoken texts in succession can make the concept more comprehensible – not necessarily watching the speeches in full, but discussing and agreeing on the tone of each speaker can reinforce the idea. Students could try and read Malala Yousafzai's autobiography and write a summary of her life so far. They could collate some quotations from her or create a collage of images and media coverage.

2 Crime and consequences

Chapter overview

This chapter introduces students to a diverse range of texts linked to the topic of crime and its consequences. Units 1–4 focus on the genre of crime fiction and its conventions, building on students' prior knowledge of the genre acquired either through study at KS2, their own reading or exposure to crime fiction in other media. It explores a variety of texts, focusing on why crime fiction is so popular, the evolution of great detective characters, how writers use narrative voices for different effects, and how writers create tension and suspense. Concepts such as genre and associated conventions, presentation of character, narrative voice, implicit meanings, narrative arc and structural techniques are embedded within Units 1–4.

Units 5–8 move away from crime fiction and look at how crime is reported in news articles; how poems can convey a criminal's perspective; how recounts of prisoners paying the penalty for their crimes can be compared; and how an editorial can be effective in shaping people's perceptions about crime. These units help to build on the knowledge that students covered in Chapter 1 Units 5–8 about perspective, tone and voice and will prepare them for what they will learn in Chapter 3.

All of the units help students to develop reading, writing and speaking and listening skills, increasing their awareness of how writers make careful choices in language, structure and form for specific effects.

This chapter builds on the foundations established at KS2 as well as the knowledge covered in Chapter 1 and continues to prepare students for the demands of the curriculum in terms of both skills and language that are required for language and literature at KS4.

Texts

The texts in this chapter provide diverse reading experiences for students. The crime fiction texts include extracts from children's and adult novels from the 19th, 20th and 21st centuries. From classic writers such as Edgar Allan Poe, to contemporary novelists such as Kim Slater and Fleur Hitchcock, students delve into key extracts and explore the writers' skills. Students should be encouraged to share any crime, mystery or detective fiction that they have enjoyed, which might include books such as *Emil and the Detectives* by Erich Kästner, *Murder Most Unladylike* by Robin Stevens, Nancy Springer's *Enola Holmes* mysteries, and their knowledge of Sir Arthur Conan Doyle's famous detective Sherlock Holmes, and the many spin-off versions of that classic series.

In terms of non-fiction texts relating to crime and its consequences, students should gain confidence in understanding news reports about crime, exploring recounts of prisoners and persuasive editorial pieces that provoke debate and encourage students to express their own views with care and consistency. During the course of this topic, students should be encouraged to share other non-fiction texts relating to crime and its consequences in newspapers, magazines, books and appropriate online sources. This chapter aims to equip students to analyse and evaluate such texts, and to craft their own texts and present them with confidence and skill.

Key

- Kerboodle
- Audio
- Reading skill
- Writing skill
- Speaking and listening skill
- **WS** Worksheet

2A Crime and consequences		
Unit	**Texts**	**Objectives**
1 Why do we love crime fiction?	• 'Four Reasons We Love Binging Crime Shows' Ekua Hagan • *Whodunit?* Philip Pullman **WS**	• Learn about the genre of crime fiction • Identify genre conventions and explore how they impact on the reader • Write a plan for your own crime story
2 What makes a character?	• 'The Murders in the Rue Morgue' Edgar Allan Poe • *Enola Holmes: The Case of the Missing Marquess* Nancy Springer **WS**	• Learn about the techniques writers use to present characters • Explore explicit and implicit information • Analyse how a character is presented
3 Who's telling the story?	• *Smart* Kim Slater • *The Complete Adventures of Feluda* Satyajit Ray **WS**	• Learn to identify and analyse narrative voices • Explore the effect of different narrative voices on the reader • Create your own narrative voice
4 Why all the tension?	• *Murder in Midwinter* Fleur Hitchcock • *The ABC Murders* Agatha Christie **WS**	• Learn about the techniques used to create tension and suspense • Explore structural and narrative devices and their effect on the reader • Comment on how a writer creates tension and suspense
Checkpoint Assessment: Chapter 2 Checkpoint 1 reading assessment; Chapter 2 Checkpoint 1 writing assessment		

2B Crime and consequences		
Unit	**Texts**	**Objectives**
5 What's the news?	• Article by Laura Mowat *Express Online* • The orange boy letter *The Times* **WS**	• Learn about the structure and features of a news report • Identify the writer's perspective and how it is presented • Write your own crime report
6 What is figurative language?	• 'Stealing' Carol Ann Duffy • 'Guilty Conscience' Sagar Garg • *Mic Drop: A High-Rise Mystery* Sharna Jackson **WS**	• Learn to identify and consider the effects of figurative language • Explore how figurative language can be used to express a perspective • Evaluate the effects of figurative language in a poem
7 What's the difference?	• *A Day in the Life of a Prisoner* Michael Romero • *My Fifteen Lost Years* Florence Maybrick • A prison account by Jessica Kent **WS** • 'Voices from Solitary' Cesar Francisco Villa **WS**	• Learn to compare texts • Summarise and synthesise the main points of two texts • Compare how writers present their perspectives
8 Can a text change your mind?	• 'Who should get credit for declining youth crime? Young people, of course' Ally Fog *The Independent* • Michael Howard's speech on crime **WS**	• Learn to identify methods used to communicate attitudes and perspectives • Explore techniques to make your perspective persuasive • Write and present a contribution to a debate
Checkpoint Assessment: Chapter 2 Checkpoint 2 writing assessment; Chapter 2 Checkpoint 2 reading assessment		

Background knowledge

Crime fiction encompasses a variety of genres, including detective fiction, espionage novels and mystery thrillers. The rise of detective fiction is linked to changes brought about by the Industrial Revolution in the late 18th and early 19th centuries, when great numbers of people moved to cities for work. Rising crime rates in these densely populated communities led to the establishment of police forces in towns and cities to uphold law and order. One of the first detectives to feature in fiction was Monsieur Dupin in Edgar Allan Poe's short story 'The Murders in the Rue Morgue', published in 1841. The first detective novel was Wilkie Collins' *The Moonstone,* published in 1868. Sir Arthur Conan Doyle published 'A Study in Scarlet' in 1887, introducing the now world-famous detective character Sherlock Holmes.

The 1920s and 1930s became known as the Golden Age of Detective Fiction. Agatha Christie published the first of her 66 detective novels in the 1920s, many of them featuring clever sleuths Hercule Poirot and Miss Marple. Novels in this genre featured crimes that the detectives (and readers) could crack by gathering clues and solving puzzles. Backlash against this type of well-ordered, neatly planned crime novel emerged in the USA, focusing on more realistic crimes, sometimes involving corrupt police and networks of organised crime. One of the most famous of these 'hardboiled crime' novels is *The Big Sleep* by Raymond Chandler (1939), featuring the tough, solitary private detective Philip Marlowe.

As well as inspiring the whole genre of crime fiction, crime and its consequences have long been a topic of ongoing public concern and interest, as reflected by macabre ballads and 'penny dreadfuls' historically, and the ongoing flow of 'true crime' articles, biographies, recounts, documentaries and online material in the present day. This chapter aims to increase students' awareness of these forms, give them the skills to engage with such texts reflectively, and the confidence to write their own.

Cross-curricular links

The selected texts link with several other areas of the curriculum, particularly History, such as Edgar Allan Poe's Victorian setting for 'The Murders in the Rue Morgue', and Florence Maybrick's account of prison life in the 19th century. Issues relating to crime and its consequences, such as social responsibility and personal wellbeing, have links to aspects of the PSHE curriculum in Year 7. Use these links to draw on students' wider and prior knowledge to make relevant connections that will deepen their understanding of these issues.

Representation and inclusion

The broad range of texts aims to foster a sense of self-confidence and self-esteem as students see aspects of themselves and their peers represented in writing, in terms of their age, gender, ethnicity, and possible experiences of or insight into crime and its consequences. Texts offer a variety of perspectives, such as that of the neuro-diverse narrator who is the sleuth in *Smart* by Kim Slater; the perpetrator of a terrible deed in Sagar Garg's poem 'Guilty Conscience'; the persona of the frustrated and bored criminal in Carol Ann Duffy's poem 'Stealing'; the autobiographical extracts from prisoners paying the price of their crimes with incarceration; and the strong, independent first-person narrator in the extract from Nancy Springer's *Enola Holmes* series.

The units offer opportunities to foster greater understanding of the benefits of diversity for society, as well as within the classroom and in the study of language and literature, enabling teachers to ensure the issues are directly relevant to the context in which their students live.

Kerboodle texts

Several alternative routes are offered on Kerboodle, so students can follow the same learning objectives in each unit while focusing on text choices that best suit their ability profile or interests. The texts range across several centuries, reflecting both male and female perspectives, as well as different cultural views, including *The Complete Adventures of Feluda* by Satyajit Ray and *Mic Drop: A High-Rise Mystery* by Sharna Jackson.

Assessment

Mini-checkpoint quizzes can be completed by students after each unit.

Spelling, punctuation and grammar mini-checkpoint quizzes can also be completed after every two units. These quizzes can be used to reinforce learning that students acquired in Year 6 or be used to support any spelling, punctuation and grammar lessons that are being undertaken in Year 7.

Checkpoint assessments are available to students after every fourth unit, after each part of the chapter. These assess students' knowledge, and skills are based on the core skills in the Quest assessment levels.

Further reading

The books and playscript below will complement the units in Chapter 2 and could be used in whole-class reading, as a class reader or in a drama session.

The Rollercoaster titles have online resource packs which will be useful when planning.

Rollercoaster *Enola Holmes*: *The Case of the Missing Marquess* Nancy Springer

Super-Readable Rollercoaster *I am the Minotaur* Antony McGowan

National Theatre Playscript *Emil and the Detectives* Erich Kästner

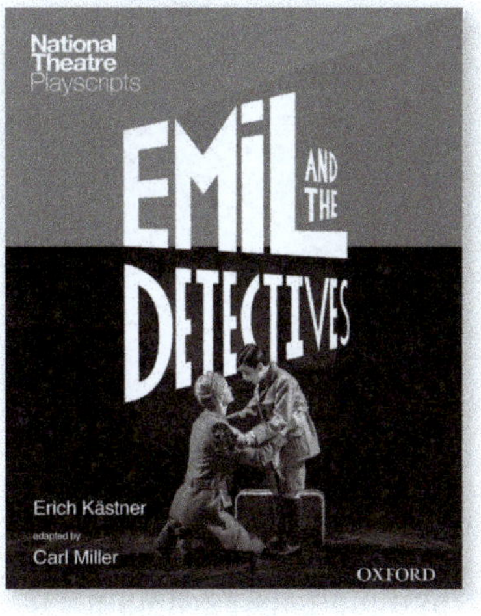

Chapter openers

How to use the chapter openers

The chapter openers include an introduction to the units with some questions to prompt students to think about the topic and to recall prior learning. The second part of the chapter opener is a learning overview that will show the route students will take through the chapter.

The chapter opener will help prepare students in understanding the texts covered in the units. It can be used to initiate a discussion about what students think might be covered in the chapter and to explore any background knowledge they have or might need to have. It can also be used to help students review their understanding at the end of the chapter and discuss what they have learned.

Encourage students to read the introduction individually or as a whole class. Discuss what crime fiction stories students are aware of, how often they read news articles about crime, what they know about punishments for crime – historically and nowadays, etc.

These activities can be done individually or as a whole-class activity alongside a general discussion about the topic to help with any background knowledge students might need.

Key vocabulary: tragedy, consequences, supernatural, intrigue, motive, suspects, reasoning, investigation, mystery, murder, detective, suspense, tension, convention, exposition, resolution

Key vocabulary

The vocabulary introduced in this chapter is linked specifically to the genre of crime fiction and analysis of non-fiction texts and poetry focusing on crime and its consequences.

Students may have met some of this vocabulary during KS1 and KS2. However, some students may struggle to visualise the more abstract concepts. Visual reminders on classroom wall displays may help, as well as providing definitions to reinforce the meanings.

Metacognition

The chapter openers provide students with a broad range of stimuli to activate their prior knowledge and experience. The prompts are both visual and text-based, with images to engage students in the issues and themes relevant to the topic itself. Text boxes provide questions designed to engage students with thought-provoking ideas.

The activities in this chapter set out to make the implicit, explicit: to draw out what many students will already intuitively know but are not necessarily aware of knowing. The activities probe students' understanding and bring to the surface key ideas and concepts relating to written and spoken texts.

Make sure that students read about how to use these pages. Encourage students to review these pages before starting a new unit.

Use the statements in these boxes to review their learning when they finish a unit and to introduce the next unit.

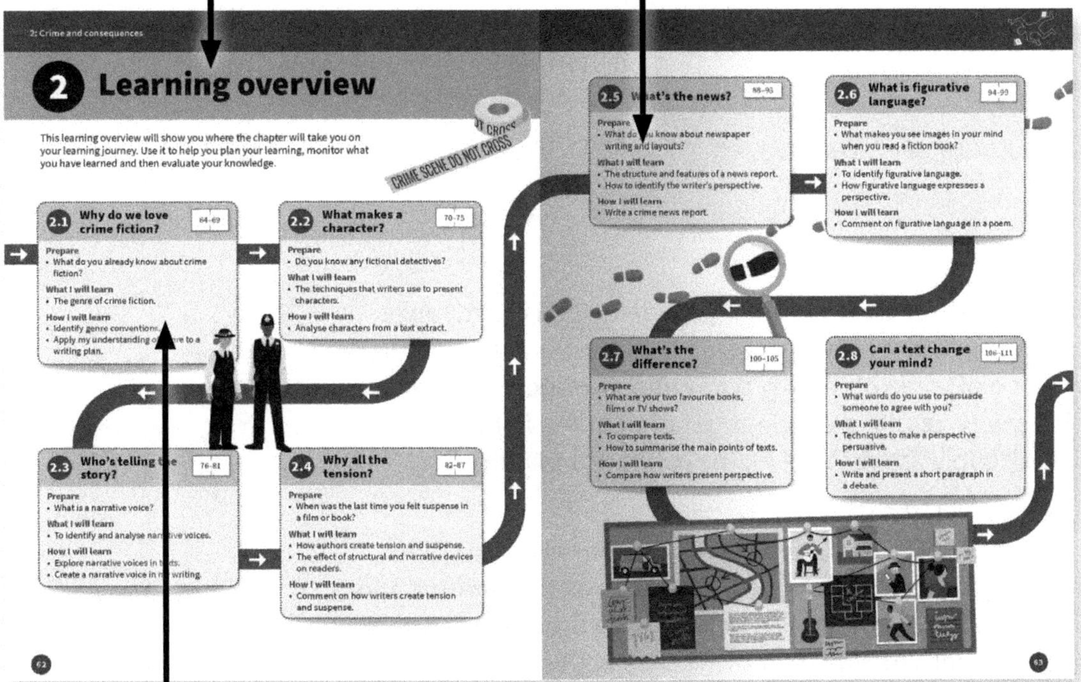

2: Crime and consequences

2 Learning overview

This learning overview will show you where the chapter will take you on your learning journey. Use it to help you plan your learning, monitor what you have learned and then evaluate your knowledge.

2.1 Why do we love crime fiction? 64–69
Prepare
• What do you already know about crime fiction?
What I will learn
• The genre of crime fiction.
How I will learn
• Identify genre conventions.
• Apply my understanding ... to a writing plan.

2.2 What makes a character? 70–75
Prepare
• Do you know any fictional detectives?
What I will learn
• The techniques that writers use to present characters.
How I will learn
• Analyse characters from a text extract.

2.3 Who's telling the story? 76–81
Prepare
• What is a narrative voice?
What I will learn
• To identify and analyse narrative voices.
How I will learn
• Explore narrative voices in texts.
• Create a narrative voice in my writing.

2.4 Why all the tension? 82–87
Prepare
• When was the last time you felt suspense in a film or book?
What I will learn
• How authors create tension and suspense.
• The effect of structural and narrative devices on readers.
How I will learn
• Comment on how writers create tension and suspense.

2.5 What's the news? 88–93
Prepare
• What do you know about newspaper writing and layouts?
What I will learn
• The structure and features of a news report.
• How to identify the writer's perspective.
How I will learn
• Write a crime news report.

2.6 What is figurative language? 94–99
Prepare
• What makes you see images in your mind when you read a fiction book?
What I will learn
• To identify figurative language.
• How figurative language expresses a perspective.
How I will learn
• Comment on figurative language in a poem.

2.7 What's the difference? 100–105
Prepare
• What are your two favourite books, films or TV shows?
What I will learn
• To compare texts.
• How to summarise the main points of texts.
How I will learn
• Compare how writers present perspective.

2.8 Can a text change your mind? 106–111
Prepare
• What words do you use to persuade someone to agree with you?
What I will learn
• Techniques to make a perspective persuasive.
How I will learn
• Write and present a short paragraph in a debate.

62

63

The statements in these boxes will help prepare students for what they will be learning in each unit. Discuss them in order to prepare students for anything that they might find challenging.

2.1 Why do we love crime fiction?

Student Book pp 64–69

Unit focus

Objectives

Students will:

- learn about the genre of crime fiction
- identify genre conventions and explore how they impact on the reader
- write a plan for their own crime story.

Unit texts

- 'Four Reasons We Love Binging Crime Shows' Ekua Hagan
- *Whodunit?* Philip Pullman **WS**

Assessment

2.1 Mini-checkpoint quiz

Key terms

- **audience** the people or person for whom a text is written or performed
- **character** a person in a drama or story
- **climax** when the action is at its most exciting or interesting
- **convention** a typical feature you find in a particular genre
- **fiction** a narrative that is imaginary or invented
- **genre** a type of story, e.g. *horror, romance, adventure, science fiction*
- **setting** where the action takes place
- **synonym** a word or phrase that means the same, or almost the same, as another word or phrase
- **text** any form of written material

Introduction to the unit

Unit 2.1 *Why do we love crime fiction?* starts by reminding students of a broad range of fiction genres, before focusing on crime fiction in particular. It looks at the history of crime fiction and the evolution of some of the key conventions associated with the genre. The source text explores why people are so fascinated by crime fiction: the excitement, the horror at what people are capable of, the mystery and ultimately the restoration of justice.

Students then share their own knowledge of crime stories, whether in books, films, plays, games or on TV, identifying key conventions of the genre in all these forms and recognising why they are so appealing. The activities build up to a final task in which students use their knowledge and skills to plan their own crime fiction story.

Activities

Starter activity

'Crime fiction' could be written on the board and students could work in pairs to write a definition to explain this term. They are likely to understand that 'fiction' means 'stories', but the word 'crime' may take more thought. Explain that the word 'crime' comes from the Latin word *crimen* meaning 'offence', and draw out that crime usually refers to a serious offence, especially one that breaks the law. It can also be used informally to mean 'a pity' or 'a shame', e.g. *It would be a crime to waste these tickets*. Before the next lesson, students could think of one crime story they have read or watched and be prepared to talk about it in groups.

Activity 1

This activity will activate prior knowledge and develop self-awareness by prompting students to consider what they already know about different fiction genres and their conventions. Students think about examples of stories they know, then decide how they would categorise them. It may be helpful to explain that some stories cover more than one genre. A summary of the class's work could be drawn up for a wall display, and examples of stories from each genre added as students progress through the term.

Kerboodle
The following activities can be replaced by the text and activities on 2.1 *Whodunit?* worksheet.

Activity 2 Boosting your vocabulary
Students explore the meaning of the word 'stimulate', linking it to the idea of making something more lively or active. It could be useful to link to words with a similar root, such as the nouns 'stimulant' and 'stimulus', and to discuss how feelings can be stimulated by what we see, hear or read – leading on to the feelings triggered by the types of texts listed. Students will need to think carefully about the similarities and differences between the words 'stimulate' and 'intrigue', drawing out the nuances of each. Discussion of the term 'taboo' will need careful handling, as some students may offer ideas about sensitive topics that could cause unease to others.

Activity 3
This activity can be used to assess students' comprehension of different paragraphs within the source text, as well as their summarising skills. It may help to model by reading through, then summarising the first paragraph, picking out key words and ideas. The subheadings give guidance, but students should use their own words. Part b may benefit from some discussion before students arrive at their final answers, exploring how some feelings can have positive and negative aspects, depending on their intensity and complexity. For example, we are often fascinated by and attracted to 'bad' ideas which can also trigger horror and repulsion.

Stretch yourself
The open-ended stretch activity challenges students to consider a controversial statement about the link between witnessing or reading about crime and the reality of committing criminal acts. Students express their own opinions first, and then focus on what the author of the article might say, backing up their arguments with evidence from the text.

Activity 4 Building your knowledge
Students could work on this activity in pairs or small groups, discussing the list of conventions first, to ensure they all understand each feature. Students should think of an example of each convention, either from what they have read or watched, or from their imagination. Once understanding is secure, they can focus on the images in the Student Book, perhaps supplemented with other available examples, e.g. film trailers, book covers, posters.

Activity 5 Building your knowledge
Before the activity, students could discuss what they know about blurbs, e.g. the purpose of blurbs. Students who need more support might benefit from a demonstration of how to read, think about and respond to one of them, making links between the conventions and the information in the blurbs. It could be useful to demonstrate how to change some vocabulary and sentence constructions to make the response more concise and fluent. More confident students can be challenged to write their own blurb about a familiar crime fiction story (or one in their imagination), highlighting evidence of genre conventions.

Activity 6 Putting it all together
Students need to be imaginative in their crime story plans, including details that are personal to them, for example by using familiar settings, and characters with similar backgrounds to their own. The detective character in particular could reflect some of their own personal traits, or those of people they know or admire. In part b students share plans with partners, and offer positive and constructive comments and suggestions, as well as perhaps pointing out one area for improvement. Some students may benefit from additional support in the form of some ideas to select from, if they struggle to think of their own.

Additional activities
Invite students to choose their own crime fiction story to talk about and present to the class or a small group. They could show a copy of the book or a short video clip, or even enact a short scene and refer to the conventions of crime fiction, describing the detective, their assistant (if relevant), the setting, the crime, the suspects and how the truth is uncovered.

2.2 What makes a character?

Student Book pp 70–75

Unit focus

Objectives

Students will:

- learn about the techniques writers use to present characters
- explore explicit and implicit information
- analyse how a character is presented.

Unit texts

- 'The Murders in the Rue Morgue' Edgar Allan Poe
- *Enola Holmes: The Case of the Missing Marquess* Nancy Springer **WS**

Assessment

2.2 Mini-checkpoint quiz

Key terms

- **antonym** a word that has the opposite meaning of a particular word
- **characterisation** the methods an author uses to create a character, e.g. describing how they look, the use of dialogue or showing how they treat others
- **connotation** an idea or feeling linked to a word, as well as its main meaning
- **dialogue** words spoken by characters
- **explicit** stating something openly and exactly
- **implicit** not stated directly, but suggested or hinted at
- **infer** to work something out from what is seen, said or done, even though it is not stated directly
- **metaphor** a comparison that says one thing *is* something else, e.g. *Amy was a rock*
- **narrator** a person who tells a story, especially in a book, play or film

Introduction to the unit

Unit 2.2 *What makes a character?* encourages students to explore the techniques that writers use to present clear, convincing and engaging portrayals of characters. As well as understanding how information can be conveyed explicitly, students explore how writers imply additional information about a character, relying on the connotation of words and the intelligence of the reader to infer additional details. The final activity gives students the opportunity to utilise their knowledge and skills to analyse aspects of a particular character, using evidence from the text and embedding quotations in their responses.

Activities

Starter activity

Ask students to choose a favourite fictional book character. They should choose a character that they feel has most impact on them; they do not have to be the hero or main character in a story. Students can write some brief notes about why they like this character, and what makes them stand out in their memory, thinking about their appearance (physical characteristics as well as clothes); how they speak; how they interact with others; what qualities make them admirable, endearing or memorable; and finally what they do or how they behave. Students then give a brief summary of their chosen character to a small group or to the class.

Activity 1

These questions activate students' prior knowledge of fictional detectives and some of their conventional characteristics, drawing from detectives in novels, comics, plays, films or TV series and giving reasons for their ideas. For example, they may feel that a great detective has to be very curious in order to want to work out the truth. They might also need to be single-minded, so that they don't get distracted by all the information they are given and all the people who try to influence them. In responding to part b of the activity, encourage students to look back at the conventions of crime fiction listed in Unit 2.1.

Kerboodle
The following activities can be replaced by the text and activities on 2.2 *Enola Holmes* worksheet.

Activity 2 Boosting your vocabulary
If necessary, remind students of the meaning of the words 'synonym' and 'antonym', giving examples, and asking students to suggest their own. Students need to understand that although the words 'cold' and 'distant' have negative connotations in this context, they do not necessarily reveal all there is to know about the character. For example, someone who appears 'cold' might actually be very shy, sensitive or unable to show their emotions. Someone who appears 'distant' might simply be preoccupied with other thoughts, rather than actually being unfriendly. Explore other words that contain the root word 'reason', e.g. 'reasonable' (adjective), 'reasonably' (adverb), 'reasonableness' (noun), encouraging students to use them accurately in sentences.

Activity 3
The first part of this activity links students' reading with what they learned in Unit 2.1 about the conventions of crime writing. The second part encourages students to think more deeply about the value of the qualities Dupin is displaying. Students will need to be able to find implicit information in the text, so make sure that they are secure in their understanding of the key terms 'implicit', 'explicit' and 'infer'. It might be helpful if students were to read the teaching text in the Building your knowledge section before Activity 3. Students may find it helpful to talk to a partner about their ideas before sharing them with the class or writing them down. Students who need more support may be guided towards thinking about what sort of work a detective does, before considering the skills that a good detective might need.

Activity 4 Building your knowledge
Students need secure understanding of the key terms 'implicit', 'explicit' and 'infer' before they read the mini-source text. Students might benefit from working in pairs that combine a more confident student and a less confident student, so that less confident students can first identify the explicit information, then more confident student discuss with their partner what additional information they can infer from the description. Students could also be directed to look at their answers in Activity 3 and think about what strategies they used to find the implied meanings. When pairs offer their responses, they need to explain what they have inferred, with close reference to the text (i.e. their ideas should not be just guesswork or assumptions, but linked to clues given in the text).

Activity 5 Building your knowledge
If possible, show students an enlarged copy of the table and talk through the characterisation techniques in the first column to secure their understanding. The definitions of 'dialogue' and 'metaphor' may need particular attention. This table could be adapted to focus on another detective in another extract, using similar characterisation techniques. The identification of the techniques is only part of the task. The second part is to think carefully about what impression or effect these techniques create for the reader.

Activity 6 Putting it all together
The final task draws together the learning from this unit, giving students the opportunity to write an extended response, but with step-by-step guidance. With students, discuss a checklist of what a successful response would include, for example, the student has: focused on the question; used quotations from the text; explained what the evidence suggests or implies about Dupin. Then they could swap their first drafts with a partner and use the checklist to give feedback. Encourage students to give at least two positive comments about their partner's work and highlight one area that might be improved. Allow sufficient time for students to complete a final draft of their work. After students have finished their final draft, they could be asked to consider if the planning table helped them with the task and to identify why or why not.

Additional activities
Challenge students to research and write about a detective (or group of detectives) in a crime fiction novel (for adults or children), providing some examples, e.g. Hercule Poirot, Emil, Precious Ramotswe, Lemony Snicket, Nancy Drew, Turtle Wexler, Sherlock Holmes, The Red Blazer Girls, The Hardy Boys, Miss Marple, Enola Holmes. Encourage students to find out what qualities make these characters super-sleuths!

2.3 Who's telling the story?

Student Book pp 76–81

Unit focus

Objectives

Students will:

- learn to identify and analyse narrative voices
- explore the effect of different narrative voices on the reader
- create their own narrative voice.

Unit texts

- *Smart* Kim Slater
- *The Complete Adventures of Feluda* Satyajit Ray **WS**

Assessment

2.3 Mini-checkpoint quiz

Key terms

- **first-person narrative** a story told by someone as if they were involved in the events themselves, using first-person pronouns, e.g. *I* and *we*
- **inciting incident** the event that sets up the action for the rest of the story
- **narrative voice** the perspective (viewpoint) from which a story is told, and the style in which it is told
- **quotation** a word or phrase from a text
- **register** the manner of speaking or writing, which can range between formal and informal
- **third-person narrative** a story told by someone who was not involved in the events themselves, using third-person pronouns, e.g. *he, she, they*
- **tone** the writer's feeling or attitude expressed towards their subject; in fiction it can also reflect a character's feelings and personality
- **unreliable narrator** a narrator who may or may not prove to be trustworthy, either intentionally or otherwise
- **verb** a word or group of words that express an action, event or state, e.g. the boy *eats*, tigers *prowl*, the building *exists*

Introduction to the unit

Unit 2.3 *Who's telling the story?* explores how a writer chooses to tell their story, through a particular perspective and using a specific tone and register. These choices affect the way a reader understands and feels about the characters. Drawing attention to these choices helps students to analyse the creation of a narrative voice and reveals the choices that they can make when writing their own stories.

Activities

Starter activity

Display the words 'narrative voice'. Ask students to discuss this phrase with a partner and write down what it means, in just one minute. If they need support, remind them that a narrative is a story. Discuss the definitions, guiding students towards understanding that it is the voice that writers create to tell their story. Read the opening sentences of stories that have a distinctive narrative voice, e.g. *I Capture the Castle* by Dodie Smith, *A Monster Calls* by Patrick Ness/Siobhan Dowd and *Wonder* by R.J. Palacio.

Ask: *Is a character talking? Is the narrator looking in on the action? What can you tell about the narrator?*

Activity 1

Students reflect on stories that they have read which have a memorable narrative voice, for example *Diary of a Wimpy Kid* (Jeff Kinney) or *Holes* (Louis Sachar). Discuss why students remember these 'voices'. Were they funny, serious, young and innocent, older and cynical, informal? Before students complete part b of the activity, check their understanding of vocabulary such as 'grave', 'opinionated', 'judgemental'.

Kerboodle

The following activities can be replaced by the text and activities on 2.3 *The Complete Adventures of Feluda* worksheet.

Activity 2 Boosting your vocabulary

Parts a and b encourage students to think beyond the most obvious meaning of the verbs and to think carefully about other ideas that are often associated with these words. Awareness of connotations and nuances of vocabulary should be developed throughout KS3 and beyond, so that students bring personal interpretations to their analysis of texts, and also make careful vocabulary choices in their own writing. Parts c and d focus on the difference between formal and informal vocabulary choices. Ensure students understand the difference, as this is built upon during further analysis of the text.

Activity 3 Building your knowledge

This activity explores, in more depth, the difference between a first- and third-person narrative, and the different effects they can create for the reader. If appropriate, introduce the concept of a second-person narrative, where the narrator uses the pronoun 'you' when describing events, e.g. 'You suspect the sound is just a branch tapping on the window, but then you catch sight of a blurry face peering through the glass…' Point out that this is an unusual form of narrative voice, but one that students should be aware of. For more confident students, introduce the concept of the 'omniscient narrator' – an all-knowing narrator who can judge events from a wide, detached perspective, for example in the opening of *A Tale of Two Cities* (Charles Dickens).

Activity 4 Building your knowledge

Before students respond to the questions, ensure their understanding of 'tone' and 'register' is secure. These concepts are sometimes confused, but ought to be revisited throughout KS3 and beyond, so that students are confident in using and discussing both concepts. Reminding students of their work on tone in Units 1.6 and 1.8 might be helpful.

Stretch yourself

Some students may have already picked up on the fact that Kieran's 'voice' is unusual and idiosyncratic, in that he doesn't seem to immediately understand what he is seeing and feels the need to explain things that may be obvious to other people. These observations (and those made in Activity 5) need to be handled sensitively.

Activity 5 Building your knowledge

This activity guides students to explore how the first-person narrative voice reveals a great deal about the character of Kieran. Students could be reminded about inference skills that they used in the previous unit. The fact that Kieran uses techniques to control his reactions suggests that he has had to learn to regulate these. His very literal interpretation of the police officer's address to him as 'son' shows that he does not recognise the meaning of this colloquial use of language. His decision to conduct a 'test' implies that he is more comfortable with methodical, rational approaches to life, rather than having an instinctive, intuitive understanding of events. These observations may lead on to a more general discussion about diversity in how people interact with the world around them. The term 'neurodiversity' could be used if appropriate. Ensure students understand that this term simply refers to the fact that people think in different ways.

Activity 6 Putting it all together

This activity draws on knowledge gained from the first three units in this chapter, giving students the opportunity to create their own detective character, using typical genre conventions and choosing a particular narrative voice. Students will need to consider how to characterise their detective, what sort of register and tone to employ in their narrative voice, and how these choices will affect the reader's experience. Before writing the paragraph, students can be encouraged to list success criteria about what they think they would need to include, e.g. clear narrative voice, description of the crime scene and the reaction of the characters.

Additional activities

Explore the concept of the 'unreliable narrator' in more detail, and the effect this may have on the reader. Do they feel cheated? Do they suspect the narrator is unreliable early on? What are the clues? Also consider the use of multiple narrators in telling a story, e.g. *Wuthering Heights* by Emily Brontë. This idea could be turned into a practical role-play activity, with students playing different characters who witness the same event but each recount a different part of it.

2.4 Why all the tension?

Student Book pp 82–87

Unit focus

Objectives

Students will:

- learn about the techniques used to create tension and suspense
- explore structural and narrative devices and their effect on the reader
- comment on how a writer creates tension and suspense.

Unit texts

- *Murder in Midwinter* Fleur Hitchcock
- *The ABC Murders* Agatha Christie **WS**

Assessment

2.4 Mini-checkpoint quiz; Chapter 2 Checkpoint 1 reading assessment; Chapter 2 Checkpoint 1 writing assessment

Key terms

- **cliffhanger** an exciting event at the end of a chapter, leaving the reader anxious and eager to know what happens next
- **contrast** to compare to show a difference
- **pace** the speed at which someone moves or something happens
- **prefix** a word or group of letters placed in front of another word to add to or change its meaning
- **suspense** a feeling of anxious uncertainty while waiting for something to happen or become known
- **tension** a feeling of being on edge with nerves stretched tight

Introduction to the unit

Unit 2.4 *Why all the tension?* explores the techniques that writers use to catch and retain the reader's attention, through their use of language, structure and narrative devices. The creation of tension and suspense is not limited to the genre of crime fiction, but it is often a very strong feature in this genre. The skills and understanding that students develop in this unit can be applied to their analysis of many different types of fiction, and also deployed in their own creative writing.

It is important that students have a secure understanding of what tension and suspense are, as these words are often used in analysis, sometimes inaccurately. Students should be able to distinguish between suspense and surprise, for example, with the former created as a sustained reaction from the reader over a period of time, but the latter as a single reaction to something unexpected.

Activities

Starter activity

Write the words 'tension' and 'suspense' on the board. Ask students to think about what these words mean and give pairs of students a piece of elastic. Explain that students need to demonstrate their literal understanding of these terms using the elastic. Guide students towards expressing 'tension' as the stretching out of the elastic until it is taut. Guide them towards demonstrating 'suspension' by hanging something from the elastic. Ask students to discuss in pairs, then explain to a group or the class, how these physical demonstrations relate to the reader's feelings while reading or watching a story. If appropriate, explain that the word 'tension' derives from the Latin word *tensum*, meaning 'stretched', and the word 'suspense' derives from the Latin words *sub* and *pendere*, meaning 'under' and 'to hang' respectively.

Activity 1

This activity should activate students' prior knowledge of the basic structure of stories. Encourage students to relate their ideas to actual stories they have read, either as children or young adults. Point out the Tip to support their answers and encourage them to use appropriate vocabulary. Guide students to draw on their understanding of the terms 'tension' and 'suspense' from the Starter activity to apply these terms to the crime fiction genre. Check that their understanding of the concept of a 'cliffhanger' is secure.

Kerboodle

The following activities can be replaced by the text and activities on 2.4 *The ABC Murders* worksheet.

Activity 2 Boosting your vocabulary

The early questions in this activity will increase students' awareness of how careful choices of vocabulary can create dramatic contrasts for the reader. The activity could be extended by using other contrasting pairs of concepts, such as heat and cold, loud and quiet sounds, dark and light. Ensure students understand that building up the emphasis on one aspect, then puncturing it with a contrast clearly focuses the reader's attention, homing in on the change. The final task in this activity provides an opportunity for students to expand their vocabulary, using a thesaurus to discover less familiar words and explore their nuances.

Activity 3 Building your knowledge

This activity builds on students' work in Activity 1. It explores story structure in more detail, using visual representation to help understanding of the crescendo of action and tension, leading to a climax, then resolution. It may be helpful to plot the development of a story the class is familiar with (not necessarily crime fiction) onto a similar graph, showing how they correlate.

Activity 4 Building your knowledge

This activity gives students an opportunity to use the questioning technique in their own creative writing. Point out that the questions in the example text also convey information for the reader. It may be helpful to model writing an example of a scene in front of the class, thinking aloud during the creative process, trying out different ideas and refining the best ones. This demonstrates the need to redraft work and dispels the common misconception that a writer's work just flows without consideration.

Activity 5 Building your knowledge

Before tackling this activity, students need to be secure in understanding the narrative techniques of the preceding mini-source texts: setting the scene, characters' questions and variation of pace. To reinforce understanding of these concepts, students could write their own examples to share first with a partner, and then take feedback from the whole class. If possible, give or show students copies of the table to complete. Less confident students could be given some responses to slot into the appropriate panels in the table.

Activity 6 Putting it all together

This activity gives students an opportunity to demonstrate their understanding of what they have learned in this unit and their skills in drawing their knowledge together. They can also think back to previous units and any specific phrases, sentences or vocabulary they used when writing about language in texts. Go through the example answer carefully, checking that students understand the process of identification of a technique, exploring its effect and its impact on the reader. Point out the sentence starters, particularly for students who need more support in this task. Work with students to establish success criteria for this activity, which they can use to check they are on track during the writing process. Encourage students to self-assess or peer-assess their completed work, identifying what they have done well and any aspects that require more work. This will highlight any areas that need further teaching and demonstration.

Additional activities

Students could research their own examples of writers creating tension and suspense effectively. It may be useful to offer a selection of texts for them to choose from, depending on what resources are available in the school library or online. This could form part of an extended project involving annotated source texts for classroom display, or could be adapted into a creative writing task. Offer opportunities for students to read their text selections (or written texts) aloud, and comment on why they think they are effective. The class could vote on which text provides the most tension and suspense for the reader.

2.5 What's the news?

Student Book pp 88–93

Unit focus

Objectives

Students will:

- learn about the structure and features of a news report
- identify the writer's perspective and how it is presented
- write their own crime report.

Unit texts

- Article by Laura Mowat *Express Online*
- The orange boy letter *The Times* **WS**

Assessment

2.5 Mini-checkpoint quiz

Key terms

- **adjective** a word that describes a noun
- **byline** a line at the beginning or end of a newspaper or magazine article that gives the writer's name
- **compare** judge how two or more things are similar and different
- **emotive language** word choices that create a strong emotional reaction in the reader
- **empathy** the ability to understand and share in someone else's feelings
- **headline** the title of a news article printed in large letters
- **objective** not influenced by personal feeling or opinion
- **purpose** the reason that a text is written
- **sensationalist** presented in a deliberate way to stir up excitement and interest
- **standfirst** a sentence or two beneath a headline, but before the main body of an article, which introduces what follows
- **subjective** influenced by personal feeling or opinion

Introduction to the unit

Unit 2.5 *What's the news?* explores how news reports are written, in terms of structure and style. Students will consider why news articles are structured in a specific way, in order to deliver information in terms of priority and level of detail. Students will learn to differentiate between formal, objective styles of reporting and more sensationalist, subjective reporting. This should enable students to form critical views when assessing news reports in any form of media.

Students are likely to be familiar with news articles from KS2 but this unit increases their awareness of the variety of writing styles that journalists employ, and gives them an opportunity to write their own crime report in the style of their choice.

Activities

Starter activity

Prior to the lesson, ask students to research two or three news article headlines to share with the class, noting down where each headline came from (which newspaper/website, etc.). Share the headlines, asking students which ones most effectively spark their interest and make them want to know more. Add further headlines featuring puns, humour, word play, drama and emotive language. Students can sort the headlines into those which seem to introduce serious information and those that feel likely to be written purely for entertainment. Talk about the target audiences of different newspapers and websites.

Activity 1

This activity should activate students' prior knowledge of newspaper articles. Draw out students' recollections and observations, putting right any misconceptions they may have about the work of journalists. Lead the discussion towards different styles used for different purposes, ranging from serious reporting on global issues, to light-hearted local entertainment, exploring different techniques used for different styles. Focus on crime writing and what will be of key interest to readers.

Kerboodle

The following activities can be replaced by the text and activities on 2.5 The orange boy letter worksheet.

Activity 2 Boosting your vocabulary

The questions are designed to reinforce students' understanding of the importance of word choice by writers. Emphasise that the richness and variety of the English language gives a great deal of choice between words with similar meanings, but with individual nuances and connotations. Choosing the most appropriate words to convey specific impressions is important in creating the overall tone of a non-fiction text.

Activity 3 Building your knowledge

This activity builds on the Starter activity, identifying features of the opening of a news article and exploring their effects. Guide students through the explanation of the structure of a news report, using the diagram. Students could make links to previous knowledge of fiction texts and look at the similarities and differences. If appropriate, use the term 'hierarchy' in relation to the importance of the information. Discuss why some people might only read headlines and the first part of a news article, e.g. level of time, interest and concentration available, and level of detail needed, etc. Talk about different reading approaches such as reading in detail and scanning and skimming headlines without reading any further. Encourage students to consider and evaluate these approaches in different contexts.

Activity 4 Building your knowledge

In this activity, students relate their knowledge of news article structure to the source text they have read. It could be expanded with examples of other news reports, showing how common this structure is. Discuss the value of additional features such as statistics and witness statements. Consider other possible features, such as images, subheadings, use of bold and italic, and links to other news articles (if online).

Activity 5 Building your knowledge

This activity requires students to use their imagination to create their own crime and then write a report about it. Students who require support could be given some options for items that could be stolen, locations, victims, motives and methods. The activity could be completed in pairs or small groups, so students pool their ideas and choose the best ones for their final plan.

Activity 6 Building your knowledge

Ensure students can identify the headline as 'Grown men in tears... exhibition for fun' and that they understand the standfirst immediately follows the headline. If necessary, remind them that a more objective style is likely to be shorter and simpler, for example, 'Vandals damage model railway exhibition ahead of its opening' for the headline. Expand the discussion on different types of readers and consider how the balance between entertainment and information varies for different groups of readers.

Stretch yourself

Encourage students to speculate on what type of reader the quotation has come from. Direct them to think about their preferred style of newspaper reporting and the issue of 'reliability'.

Activity 7 Putting it all together

This activity draws together all that students have learned in the unit and gives them an opportunity to write their own crime report in full. Students could be supported in creating the vocabulary bank and by a written model of the first paragraph or a demonstration of how to embed witness statements effectively in the report. When modelling, thought processes should be explicit to show how to consider, select, refine or reject ideas. Students could be encouraged to pause during their writing to spend some time re-reading and looking at any models to monitor their own writing.

Additional activities

Ask students to comment on articles about crime, discussing the structure and style.

Students could research a real crime of theft and use it to plan their own news report. They may need to make up some of the details from their imagination if all the real facts are unavailable or unknown.

2.6 What is figurative language?

Student Book pp 94–99

Unit focus

Objectives

Students will:

- learn to identify and consider the effects of figurative language
- explore how figurative language can be used to express a perspective
- evaluate the effects of figurative language in a poem.

Unit texts

- 'Stealing' Carol Ann Duffy
- 'Guilty Conscience' Sagar Garg
- *Mic Drop: A High-Rise Mystery* Sharna Jackson **WS**

Assessment

2.6 Mini-checkpoint quiz

Key terms

- **alliteration** using the same letter or sound at the beginning of several words for special effect
- **colloquial language** informal words or phrases that are suitable for ordinary conversation, rather than formal speech or writing
- **figurative language** words or phrases with a meaning that is different from the literal meaning
- **monologue** a speech by one character
- **onomatopoeia** words that imitate or suggest what they stand for, e.g. *cuckoo, sizzle*
- **repetition** using the same word or phrase more than once
- **rhetorical question** a question asked for dramatic effect and not intended to get an answer
- **simile** a comparison of one thing to another, using *as* or *like*, e.g. *He swam like a fish*
- **stanza** a group of lines in a poem with a line space before and after it
- **subject** the person or thing that does the verb, e.g. *the boy* eats, *tigers* prowl, *the building* exists

Introduction to the unit

Unit 2.6 *What is figurative language?* explores how a poet conveys the character and emotions of a narrator through figurative language. As well as learning to recognise figurative language techniques, students are guided to understand how imagery creates particular effects for the reader, beyond literal description.

This unit builds on Unit 2.3's focus on narrative voices in novels, and on Unit 2.2's focus on the creation of character. Understanding how a writer creates a persona to tell a story from a particular perspective is important as students progress through their KS3 English studies. Recognition that a created narrator is not the same person/persona as the poet or novelist themselves is fundamental to understanding the writer's craft.

Activities

Starter activity

Ask students to choose a famous fictional villain, e.g. Lord Voldemort (*Harry Potter*), Shere Khan (*The Jungle Book*), Cruella de Vil (*101 Dalmatians*), Agatha Trunchbull (*Matilda*). Briefly play 'Who am I?', inviting one student to answer 'yes' or 'no' to questions until the class guesses their identity. Keep the activity short and pacey. For the second part of the activity, students imagine they are that villain and write or say two sentences in that persona, commenting on their crimes, ambitions or attitude to other characters. Explain that this activity will help them to understand character perspectives.

Activity 1
These questions activate students' prior knowledge of figurative language. Students might find it helpful to work on their mind map in pairs, then feed back to create a whole-class mind map for display. Ensure students understand all the terms they use and can give examples. For the second part of this activity, encourage students to consider the difficulties they may encounter, and possible solutions, such as spelling strategies, practising identification of features and securing vocabulary for commenting on effects, encouraging them to have agency with their learning.

Kerboodle
The following activities can be replaced by the text and activities on 2.6 *Mic Drop: A High-Rise Mystery* worksheet.

Activity 2 Boosting your vocabulary
Discuss the vocabulary choices the poet uses, encouraging students to express and discuss their ideas. Draw out how these vocabulary choices affect the reader and convey subtle clues as to the narrator – their history, age, problems and personality. For part e, ensure students understand what colloquial language is as opposed to formal Standard English. Offer more examples and ask students to come up with their own. This should build on work covered in Chapter 1 Unit 7 *Which English do you speak?*, where students looked at code-switching and different styles of English language.

Activity 3
Students might benefit from discussing the questions in this activity with a partner, before giving a response. Check their understanding of inference is secure; if necessary remind them of work done in Unit 2.2.

Activity 4 Building your knowledge
If possible, give or show students a copy of the table to complete. Read through the instructions with the class, checking understanding. If necessary, model how to complete another row of the table, speaking aloud to demonstrate how to consider what to write, for example testing, rejecting and selecting appropriate responses. Point out the sample phrases used in student answers, adding to the bank of useful vocabulary and phrases if necessary.

Activity 5 Building your knowledge
This activity is an opportunity for students to develop a personal response to the poem. Encourage students to share their ideas with partners or in a small group and listen to other students' opinions on the poem. Some students may benefit from reminders about how to interact constructively in speaking and listening tasks.

Activity 6 Putting it all together
Ensure students read the poem at least twice before attempting to discuss the questions in this activity. If necessary, pre-teach some of the vocabulary which some students may be unfamiliar with. Talk about the detail of the figurative language. Some students may find it helpful to sketch out some of the images the poet creates, expressing the feelings created by these images.

Activity 7 Putting it all together
This activity draws together all the learning and skills covered in this unit. Although answering an exam-type question can seem daunting, remind students that they are fully equipped to respond to this question, using what they have already done in this unit. Students could discuss each skill that is required for this task and what strategies they might need to employ to support them. It may be helpful to build in a reflection time after students have written their notes, sharing them with a partner or small group, then revising them in the light of others' ideas, before writing their full response.

Additional activities
Challenge students to write their own poem about guilt, encouraging them to create a persona, rather than writing autobiographically. Encourage them to use figurative language to make the feelings dramatic and vivid for the reader. Suggest some possible scenarios for students who struggle with ideas, e.g. doing something that would upset a family member or friend. Remind students that their poem does not need to rhyme or even have a regular rhythm, but their ideas should be succinct, their vocabulary carefully chosen, and their images effective and memorable for the reader.

2.7 What's the difference?

Student Book pp 100–105

Unit focus

Objectives

Students will:

- learn to compare texts
- summarise and synthesise the main points of two texts
- compare how writers present their perspectives.

Unit texts

- *A Day in the Life of a Prisoner* Michael Romero
- *My Fifteen Lost Years* Florence Maybrick
- A prison account by Jessica Kent **WS**
- 'Voices from Solitary' Cesar Francisco Villa **WS**

Assessment

2.7 Mini-checkpoint quiz

Key terms

- **adverbial** a word or phrase that explains how, where or when something happened, or shows how ideas relate to one another
- **conjunction** a linking word, e.g. *if, and, but*
- **connective** a general term for a word or phrase that helps link information
- **non-fiction** real events or factual information
- **synthesise** to combine separate parts into something new

Introduction to the unit

Unit 2.7 *What's the difference?* gives students the opportunity to think about two texts in relation to each other, as well as individually. This skill of comparison can be challenging for students, but repeated practice throughout KS3 will build their confidence as they learn to pick out key features and facts for comparison. This unit builds on the comparison skills introduced in Chapter 1 Unit 3 *What's the story?*

The texts in this unit are both recounts by real prisoners, who were imprisoned as a consequence of their alleged crimes. (Florence Maybrick was ultimately cleared of the crime after 15 years in prison.) Students should be aware that there will always be some similar key features in texts they are comparing, either in form, subject matter or style – and possibly a mix of these. The subjects raised should be handled sensitively as students may know people who are or have been imprisoned.

Activities

Starter activity

Ask students what they know about life in prison. They may have read articles or novels about prisons and prisoners, or they may draw on stories or documentaries they have seen in other media. Draw out that some people's views may differ. Some people might believe that life in prison can be too 'easy'; others may feel it can be brutal and damaging.

Discuss how important is it that punishment is appropriate to the crime. What do they think about keeping prisoners in solitary confinement? Encourage students to write one statement about the positive effects of imprisonment and one statement about the negative effects of imprisonment.

Activity 1

Check students' understanding of the terms 'adverbials', 'conjunctions' and the umbrella term 'connectives' from KS2. Demonstrate picking out key words and phrases from a paragraph, using skimming and scanning and underlining or circling key words and phrases. Responses to part c of the activity may vary. Encourage students to talk about tone and register, as well as vocabulary choice and text structure. Students will have touched on these concepts in Chapter 1, for example in Unit 1.8 *What's the right tone?*

Kerboodle

The following activities can be replaced by the text and activities on 2.7 Accounts of imprisonment worksheet.

Activity 2 Boosting your vocabulary

This activity focuses attention on key vocabulary used in the texts, such as 'routine' and 'confined', as well as connotations of the words 'box' and 'cage'. Explore how these words reveal a lot about the prisoners' attitudes and perspectives. Students should be familiar with using the Frayer model to explore words in depth, but may need further explanation (refer back to the completed Frayer model for 'impressionable' in Unit 1.6 if helpful). Parts c–d encourage students to think about how a character such as Romero may use contrasting vocabulary to describe different parts of their life experience, leading to a more complex response from a reader towards that individual. The final section could be used to encourage students to think about how words can have different connotations, depending on their context. Some students may need more support to recognise this, in which case give them further examples of the same word being used in different contexts, each conveying a different impression.

Activity 3 Building your knowledge

Briefly check students' understanding of the terms 'similarities' and 'differences'. Ask them to use these terms in a few sentences about themselves and classmates (nothing too personal or controversial). Many students may find it easier to envisage the similarities and differences using a Venn diagram, as in the Student Book. Demonstrate this by using information about students before applying it to the texts. For students that need more support with the written task, model how to start making notes in a Venn diagram in front of the class, then encourage students to complete their diagrams in pairs or individually.

Stretch yourself

This activity encourages students to identify relevant words and phrases, and also to explain in writing how they are used for maximum effect for the reader.

Activity 4 Building your knowledge

This activity builds on Activity 3, but focuses on language techniques rather than factual content. If necessary, model identifying one language technique and explaining how and why it is used effectively. Some students might benefit from putting this information into a table, as in Unit 2.6 Activity 4.

Activity 5 Putting it all together

The final task requires students to demonstrate the knowledge and skills gained from this unit. Read the exam question together as a class and ask students what they think the key words are. Guide them to focus in particular on 'compare', 'present' and 'perspectives'. Ensure students understand what the question requires, reading through the three bullet points. The extract from one student's answer should be read and discussed, along with the teacher's comments. Check students' understanding of the comments, drawing out the two positive points and one suggestion for improvement. It may be useful to introduce a first draft stage into this writing task, so that there is opportunity for students to check their own work (or that of a partner) against earlier aims. Allow time for the writing of a final draft, together with time to check for spelling, grammar and punctuation.

Additional activities

Students could compare two more texts of their choice, or the two poems from Unit 2.6, using a Venn diagram to plan their ideas. Encourage them to think about how a Venn diagram has an advantage over simply listing ideas.

2.8 Can a text change your mind?

Student Book pp 106–111

Unit focus

Objectives

Students will:

- learn to identify methods used to communicate attitudes and perspectives
- explore techniques to make their perspective persuasive
- write and present a contribution to a debate.

Unit texts

- 'Who should get credit for declining youth crime? Young people, of course' Ally Fog *The Independent*
- Michael Howard's speech on crime **WS**

Assessment

2.8 Mini-checkpoint quiz; Chapter 2 Checkpoint 2 writing assessment; Chapter 2 Checkpoint 2 reading assessment

Key terms

- **anecdote** a short or entertaining story about real people or events
- **debate** to have a formal discussion in which opposite views on a subject are heard fairly
- **editorial** a newspaper article expressing a writer's opinion
- **fluency** speaking with a smooth flow, without hesitating
- **gesture** using your hands to indicate meaning, e.g. to help emphasise certain points
- **juvenile** linked to young people
- **persuasive** making you want to do or believe something
- **tricolon** a pattern of three words or phrases grouped together to be memorable and have impact

Introduction to the unit

Unit 2.8 *Can a text change your mind?* explores the techniques that writers and speakers use to persuade readers and audiences to agree with a certain perspective, building on the skills introduced in Chapter 1 Unit 6 *How is your voice heard?* and Chapter 1 Unit 8 *What's the right tone?,* which focus on the effective use of tone to influence a reader/ audience. The unit also reminds students about how to perform in a debate, presenting a perspective and delivering a speech effectively.

Activities

Starter activity

On the board, write 'Argument or Debate?'. Give students a few minutes to discuss the differences between the two with a partner, then take feedback as a whole class. Draw out that, although both involve people holding different points of view, an argument may be more emotional and personal, taking place spontaneously, while a debate is a more formal discussion, contained within a set process, with a proposal (statement), speakers for and against the proposal, a chairperson and a vote. Ask students which they think is the most effective way to persuade people of a perspective and to explain why.

Activity 1

These questions activate students' prior knowledge of persuasive techniques. Students could work in pairs and discuss how they would persuade their partner to like something that they don't currently like, e.g. a song, a meal etc. Then ask them to think about what they were doing to persuade, e.g. what language they were using and how they were speaking. It may be helpful to start off a mind map of techniques as a whole class, for students to finish independently. Add to this mind map during or at the end of the unit. The final mind map could be made into a classroom display for future reference.

Kerboodle
The following activities can be replaced by the text and activities on 2.8 Michael Howard's speech on crime worksheet.

Activity 2 Boosting your vocabulary
Before focusing on the vocabulary in the extract, ensure students are secure in understanding that an 'editorial' is written by the editor of a newspaper or news website, and usually gives a strong opinion on a current issue or event. When discussing the word 'demonised', be prepared to give a personal example, explaining the circumstances and how it felt. The word 'delinquent' could be explored further using the Frayer model, either as an adjective or a noun.

Activity 3
To activate prior knowledge, students could revisit the text in Unit 2.5 and compare the two articles from Unit 2.8 and Unit 2.5. The first part of this activity encourages students to consider the writer's perspective, to decide whether they agree with it, and to develop their own ideas and opinions, explaining their thought processes. The final part of this activity could be assessed as a mini-debating activity, but without a formal structure. Students could discuss the statement in pairs or small groups, in an informal setting. If necessary, remind students to take turns speaking, not to interrupt each other, to listen to what each other says and respond to it, as well as to try to express their own views clearly and succinctly. Observe students during their discussions, noting strengths and areas that need further work.

Activity 4 Building your knowledge
Students could be reminded about the skills needed for this task and draw upon any strategies that they learned from Activity 4 in Unit 2.6. If possible, give or show students a copy of the table to complete. Discuss the features of persuasive language covered in the text, ensuring that students' understanding of all the relevant terms is secure. Invite students to give additional examples of the techniques, used outside the text. These could be made-up or drawn from other texts or speeches. If some students need support in identifying the techniques, provide a variety of evidence and ask them to link them to the appropriate technique. If students need more support, model how to complete another row in the table, speaking the thought processes aloud, for students to emulate.

Stretch yourself
Students might pick out additional techniques, such as the use of 'we' to emphasise collective responsibility; the use of contrast, e.g. blame/applause; use of humour, e.g. reference to Eden Lake and 'young bandits'; repetition of concepts, e.g. 'truth'/'true'. Ensure they explain the impact of these techniques and how they engage and entertain the reader, and reinforce the message for the reader.

Activity 5 Building your knowledge
This activity encourages students to reflect on the qualities of an effective speaker generally, then to consider their own skills. Ranking the order of skills could be done first by pairs of students, then shared with another pair. Note that there is not a fixed correct/incorrect ranking, but the activity should give students the opportunity to think carefully about each of the skills and recognise their importance.

Activity 6 Putting it all together
The final task draws together the learning from this unit, giving students the opportunity to write and present their work in a formal debate. If necessary, remind students of the form of a formal debate. This is an opportunity to assess students' performance in the debate, in terms of the content of their speech as well as their skill in delivering it. If appropriate, invite students to assess each other (reminding them to give positive, as well as constructive feedback).

Additional activities
Ask students to find an example of a speech that they admire. It may be useful to give them some links to recordings of speeches online to choose from or direct them towards the scripts of well-known speeches. Ask them to choose their favourite speech and be prepared to explain why they think it is effective and persuasive. Allow them an opportunity to discuss/present their findings in detail.

3 Journeys and discoveries

Chapter overview

This chapter takes students on a number of journeys. Through poems, autobiography, fiction and non-fiction, they will explore the challenges and benefits of travel and the links between physical journeys – real and imagined – and metaphorical journeys of self-discovery. Chapter 3 continues to build and broaden the knowledge that students have gained from the first two chapters, using more challenging texts.

Units 1–4 focus on fiction and poetry. Students will be able to draw on their prior knowledge of texts about journeys, as well as those that use journeys as a storytelling device, including the traditional quest. They will understand how a journey can be used to create jeopardy, drawing the reader in and setting characters off on their narrative arcs. Students will then look at real journeys in poetry before, in Units 5–8, turning their attention to travel writing. Beginning with local travel and their own neighbourhoods, students will go on to look at the temptations of travel on a global level, and also consider its impact on the planet. Finally, they will read and respond to a literary account of a real-life journey at a key moment in time.

Throughout the chapter, students will have the opportunity to make connections between the reading they have done at KS2 while undertaking a range of tasks that will help to prepare them for the reading and writing demands of the rest of KS3 and KS4.

Texts

The texts in this chapter are written by novelists, travel writers, poets, journalists and autobiographers. Students will read extracts from contemporary middle-grade and Young Adult fiction, as well as texts originally written for an adult audience. Students will be supported to read and respond to extracts that are more traditional and archaic in style and syntax, such as from the novel *Jamaica Inn* by Daphne Du Maurier. Meanwhile, contemporary texts range from those that are direct and accessible, to those that resist simple reading and require more developed inference skills. Writers such as Wang Ping, Stephen King, Floella Benjamin, Jessie Burton, Jacqueline Woodson and Deborah O'Donoghue provide a range of diverse reading for students. Further reading to widen students' textual knowledge and intertextual experience is suggested on page 67.

Key

- Kerboodle
- Audio
- Reading skill
- Writing skill
- Speaking and listening skill
- **WS** Worksheet

3A Journeys and discoveries		
Unit	**Texts**	**Objectives**
1 How do journeys create jeopardy?	• *The Body* Stephen King • *Running on the Roof of the World* Jess Butterworth **WS**	• Learn how writers make deliberate choices to create a sense of danger • Explore the features of a 'coming-of-age' story • Analyse how a writer creates a sense of jeopardy in a text
2 What is a quest?	• *Medusa* Jessie Burton • *Sir Gawain and the Green Knight* Simon Armitage **WS**	• Learn to identify the main features of a quest and some other story types • Explore first-person narrative and inference • Write a scene for your own quest story, using key conventions
3 Why start with a journey?	• *Jamaica Inn* Daphne Du Maurier • *The Secret Garden* Frances Hodgson Burnett **WS**	• Learn to recognise key plot conventions • Identify word choices and literary devices and comment on their effects • Analyse the presentation of a journey, using close textual reference
4 How can poetry explore journeys?	• 'Things We Carry on the Sea' Wang Ping • 'An Escape' Ha Jin **WS**	• Learn how texts are influenced by the contexts in which they are written • Rehearse and perform a poetry reading • Recognise poetic features and comment on their effect
Checkpoint Assessment: Chapter 3 Checkpoint 1 reading assessment; Chapter 3 Checkpoint 1 writing assessment		

3B Journeys and discoveries		
Unit	**Texts**	**Objectives**
5 What is travel writing?	• Blog post on alastairhumphreys.com Alastair Humphreys • A letter from Lady Montagu **WS**	• Learn about the key conventions of travel writing • Identify the effects of grammatical features in travel writing • Write about a journey around your neighbourhood
6 Why travel sustainably?	• 'Electric road trip through Switzerland', 'Easy train to Sweden', 'Wildlife safari, Spain' in '20 of the Best Sustainable Holidays in Europe for 2020' Gemma Bowes • '7 steps to being a mindful traveller' Soraya Abdel Hadi **WS**	• Learn about features of persuasive texts • Explore the effects of persuasive techniques on the reader • Write and present a speech confidently in front of an audience
7 Why take a risk?	• 'Bungee at Victoria Falls: The Day the Void Came for Me' Deborah O'Donoghue • 'Bungee at Victoria Falls: The Day the Void Came for Me' Part 2 Deborah O'Donoghue **WS**	• Learn to recognise the effect of a writer's choice of techniques in a piece of travel writing • Explore how the structure of a piece of travel writing creates excitement • Write an article about a travel adventure
8 Can journeys tell stories?	• *Brown Girl Dreaming* Jacqueline Woodson • *Coming to England* Floella Benjamin **WS**	• Learn about the conventions of autobiographical writing • Learn how to structure an analytical response • Write about a literary text using a formal, analytical style
Checkpoint Assessment: Chapter 3 Checkpoint 2 speaking and listening assessment; Chapter 3 Checkpoint 2 writing assessment		

Background knowledge

Books and texts about journeys and discoveries have a long history, from travel guides, travel memoirs and travelogues to fictional journeys and quests. The first travel guides were written over 200 years ago and many well-known series started not long after, such as Murray's Handbooks and Baedeker Guides. The 20th century saw the rise of the Lonely Planet series for travellers who wanted to go to exotic destinations. In fiction, stories of journeys can be used as metaphors of the journey of life or as a symbol of the transition from childhood to adulthood. They can also be about self-discovery and healing. Some of the earliest stories about journeys were Ancient Greek myths, such as Odysseus's epic travels in Homer's *The Odyssey.* These stories were often quests that the main protagonist undertook, to find a mythical being or a precious object or an answer to one of life's most difficult questions. There are tests to endure and pass before arriving at the destination and the object of the quest. A quest is now a well-used plot type and familiar to many students. The *Harry Potter* series is a famous quest story, as well as the *His Dark Materials* trilogy. There are many 19th-century and early 20th-century novels that follow the quest plot, such as *Treasure Island, The Wizard of Oz* and *Lord of the Rings*.

Cross-curricular links

The selected texts link with several other areas of the curriculum, particularly History with Jessie Burton's retelling of Medusa's story. This is an opportunity to recap and extend KS2 learning about ancient civilisations, while Jacqueline Woodson's autobiography will take students to the heart of the Black Civil Rights Movement and *Coming to England* by Floella Benjamin speaks directly of the experiences of the Windrush generation. Another cross-curricular link is with Ethics and PSHE. Reading Wang Ping's 'Things We Carry on the Sea' and Ha Jin's 'An Escape' will deepen students' understanding of migration and the issues facing refugees around the world. These texts will also support discussions of related ideas, such as race, human rights and social inclusion. Finally, Unit 3.5 provides a direct link to studies of human and physical geography of the local environment. The impact of humankind on the planet and sustainable travel are another potential focus for a cross-curricular link.

Representation and inclusion

The range of texts in this chapter will complement and enrich the wider school reading curriculum, helping to ensure that all students see themselves in the books and extracts they encounter. From variations on the literary canon, such as *Medusa* by Jessie Burton, to 21st-century writing published for middle-grade readers, the texts have been selected for their broad appeal and accessibility, as well as to offer challenge. Diverse voices are represented, and students will be encouraged to respond to these in a sensitive way. Texts such as Wang Ping's 'Things We Carry on The Sea' directly address issues of migration, exploring the important common experiences of refugees and highlighting the unique stories and words of those fleeing war, persecution and environmental disaster. *Brown Girl Dreaming*, Jacqueline Woodson's autobiography in verse, reflects on the personal impact of a politically significant time.

To further broaden students' reading, invite them to bring in books in a range of the languages and scripts that they may speak or read at home. Ask other students to try to glean some meaning from the texts in the languages they do not speak or read, such as by making inferences from visual clues.

Kerboodle texts

Several alternative routes are offered on Kerboodle, so students can follow the same learning objectives in each unit while focusing on text choices that best suit their ability profile or interests. For example, in Unit 3.1, an extract from Jess Butterworth's middle-grade novel *Running on the Roof of the World* provides an accessible way to explore jeopardy, while the Student Book text *The Body* by Stephen King, offers challenge to more mature readers. The Kerboodle texts can also be used in addition to the main Student Book text, to contrast context and perspective. Compare, for instance, Lady Mary Wortley Montagu's early 18th-century travel letter with the contemporary travel blog of Alastair Humphreys. In other units, the Kerboodle texts allow students to delve more deeply into an issue – such as the pros and cons of travel and the benefits of sustainable tourism (see Unit 3.6).

Assessment

Mini-checkpoint quizzes can be completed by students after each unit.

Spelling, punctuation and grammar mini-checkpoint quizzes can also be completed after every two units. These quizzes can be used to reinforce learning that students acquired in Year 6 or be used to support any spelling, punctuation and grammar lessons that are being undertaken in Year 7.

Checkpoint assessments are available to students after every fourth unit, after each part of the chapter. These assess students' knowledge, and skills are based on the core skills in the Quest assessment levels.

Further reading

The books and playscripts below will complement the units in Chapter 3 and could be used in whole-class reading, as a class reader or in a drama session.

The Rollercoaster titles have online resource packs which will be useful when planning.

Rollercoaster *Boy, Everywhere* A.M. Dassu

Super-Readable Rollercoaster *Edgar & Adolf* Phil Earle and Michael Wagg

RSC School Shakespeare *The Tempest*

National Theatre Playscript *Treasure Island*

Chapter openers

How to use the chapter openers

The chapter openers include an introduction to the units with some questions to prompt students to think about the topic and to recall prior learning. The second part of the chapter opener is a learning overview that will show the route students will take through the chapter.

The chapter opener will help prepare students in understanding the texts covered in the units. It can be used to initiate a discussion about what students think might be covered in the chapter and to explore any background knowledge they have or might need to have. It can also be used to help students review their understanding at the end of the chapter and discuss what they have learned.

Encourage students to read the introduction individually or as a whole class. Discuss what texts they have already read in which characters go on physical journeys between places and metaphorical journeys of self-discovery.

These activities can be done individually, in pairs, or as a whole-class activity alongside a general discussion about the topic to help with any background knowledge students might need.

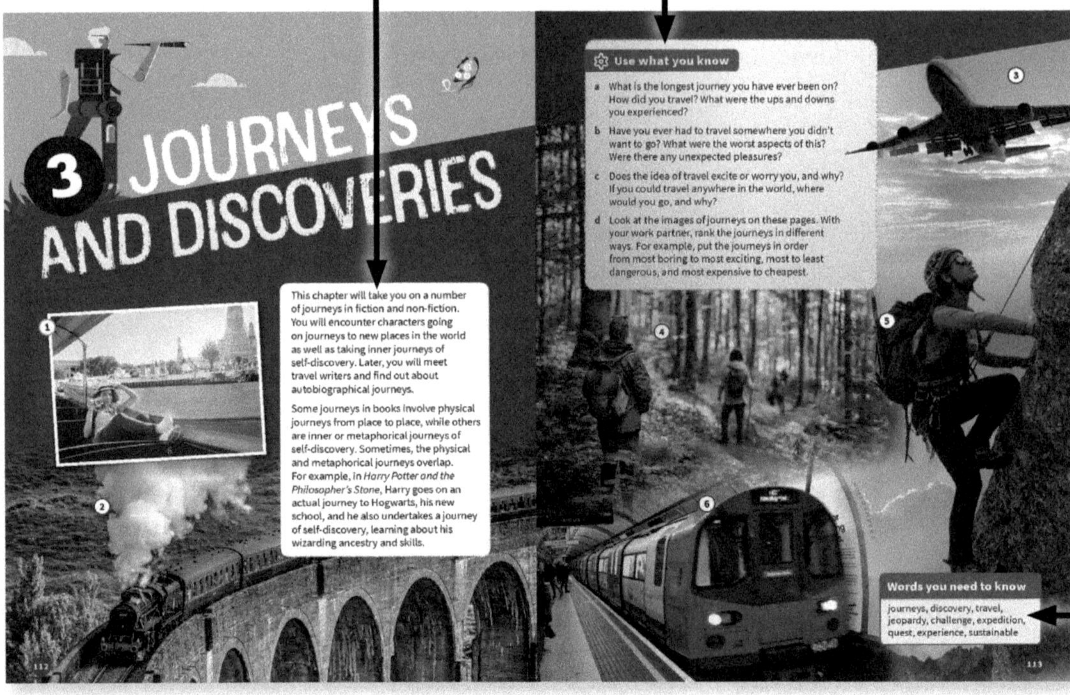

Key vocabulary: journeys, discovery, travel, jeopardy, challenge, expedition, quest, experience, sustainable

Key vocabulary

The vocabulary for this chapter will support students as they discuss texts that use journeys to tell stories and then proceed to consider the theme of travel in non-fiction. Students will have met some of this vocabulary during KS1 and KS2. However, some students may struggle to visualise the more abstract concepts. Visual reminders of key words and their definitions on classroom wall displays may help, alongside the learning overview provided to show students the direction of their learning.

Metacognition

The chapter openers provide students with a broad range of stimuli to activate their prior knowledge and experience. The prompts are both visual and text-based, with images to engage students in the issues and themes relevant to the topic itself. Text boxes provide questions designed to engage students with thought-provoking ideas.

The activities in this chapter set out to make the implicit, explicit: to draw out what many students will already intuitively know but are not necessarily aware of knowing.

The activities probe students' understanding and bring to the surface key ideas and concepts relating to written and spoken texts.

Make sure that students read about how to use these pages. Encourage students to review these pages before starting a new unit.

Use the statements in these boxes to review their learning when they finish a unit and to introduce the next unit.

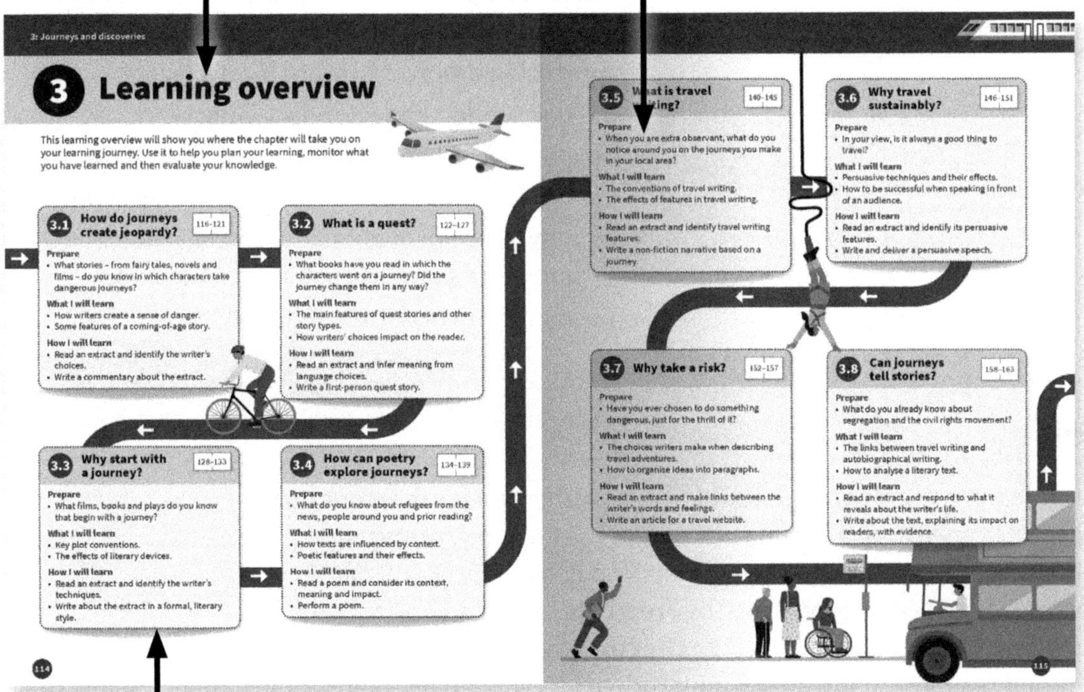
3: Journeys and discoveries

3 Learning overview

This learning overview will show you where the chapter will take you on your learning journey. Use it to help you plan your learning, monitor what you have learned and then evaluate your knowledge.

3.1 How do journeys create jeopardy? 116–121

Prepare
- What stories – from fairy tales, novels and films – do you know in which characters take dangerous journeys?

What I will learn
- How writers create a sense of danger.
- Some features of a coming-of-age story.

How I will learn
- Read an extract and identify the writer's choices.
- Write a commentary about the extract.

3.2 What is a quest? 122–127

Prepare
- What books have you read in which the characters went on a journey? Did the journey change them in any way?

What I will learn
- The main features of quest stories and other story types.
- How writers' choices impact on the reader.

How I will learn
- Read an extract and infer meaning from language choices.
- Write a first-person quest story.

3.3 Why start with a journey? 128–133

Prepare
- What films, books and plays do you know that begin with a journey?

What I will learn
- Key plot conventions.
- The effects of literary devices.

How I will learn
- Read an extract and identify the writer's techniques.
- Write about the extract in a formal, literary style.

3.4 How can poetry explore journeys? 134–139

Prepare
- What do you know about refugees from the news, people around you and prior reading?

What I will learn
- How texts are influenced by context.
- Poetic features and their effects.

How I will learn
- Read a poem and consider its context, meaning and impact.
- Perform a poem.

114

3.5 W[illegible]at is travel [illegible]ing? 140–145

Prepare
- When you are extra observant, what do you notice around you on the journeys you make in your local area?

What I will learn
- The conventions of travel writing.
- The effects of features in travel writing.

How I will learn
- Read an extract and identify travel writing features.
- Write a non-fiction narrative based on a journey.

3.6 Why travel sustainably? 146–151

Prepare
- In your view, is it always a good thing to travel?

What I will learn
- Persuasive techniques and their effects.
- How to be successful when speaking in front of an audience.

How I will learn
- Read an extract and identify its persuasive features.
- Write and deliver a persuasive speech.

3.7 Why take a risk? 152–157

Prepare
- Have you ever chosen to do something dangerous, just for the thrill of it?

What I will learn
- The choices writers make when describing travel adventures.
- How to organise ideas into paragraphs.

How I will learn
- Read an extract and make links between the writer's words and feelings.
- Write an article for a travel website.

3.8 Can journeys tell stories? 158–163

Prepare
- What do you already know about segregation and the civil rights movement?

What I will learn
- The links between travel writing and autobiographical writing.
- How to analyse a literary text.

How I will learn
- Read an extract and respond to what it reveals about the writer's life.
- Write about the text, explaining its impact on readers, with evidence.

115

The statements in these boxes will help prepare students for what they will be learning in each unit. Discuss them in order to prepare students for anything that they might find challenging.

3.1 How do journeys create jeopardy?

Student Book pp 116–121

Unit focus

Objectives

Students will:

- learn how writers make deliberate choices to create a sense of danger
- explore the features of a 'coming-of-age' story
- analyse how a writer creates a sense of jeopardy in a text.

Unit texts

- *The Body* Stephen King
- *Running on the Roof of the World* Jess Butterworth **WS**

Assessment

3.1 Mini-checkpoint quiz

Key terms

- **adverb** and **adverbial** a word or phrase that explains how, where or when something happened, or how ideas relate to one another
- **character** a person in a drama or story
- **coming-of-age story** a story in which characters experience things that teach them about adulthood
- **commentary** a written explanation or discussion
- **convention** a typical feature you find in a particular genre
- **genre** a type of story, e.g. *horror, romance, adventure, science fiction*
- **narrator** a person who tells a story, especially in a book, play or film
- **quotation** a word or phrase from a text
- **setting** where the action takes place
- **suspense** a feeling of anxious uncertainty while waiting for something to happen or become known
- **synonym** a word or phrase that means the same, or almost the same, as another word or phrase
- **text** any form of written material

Introduction to the unit

Unit 3.1 *How do journeys create jeopardy?* grabs students' attention with a literary moment that has become a classic film scene: Stephen King's description of four pre-teen boys crossing a hazardous single-line rail bridge from the coming-of-age novella *The Body* (filmed as *Stand By Me*). Students are introduced to the concept of jeopardy. They read the scene in two sections, focusing first on how character is revealed in the build-up to the crossing and then on descriptive language. Handle the reading and response sensitively if any students have been affected by crashes or other accidents. More mature and ambitious readers may enjoy the whole King story or his other fiction appropriate for a young-adult audience. However, note that the original text features some swear words and should therefore be shared with caution.

Activities

Starter activity

Copies of the spoken lines from the extract could be provided, set out as a script for four parts. Students can enact the script in groups of four, adding appropriate actions. This requires them to imagine the scenario that prompts the boys' discussion. Two or three groups could perform the scene, considering what tone of voice seems right for each line, and what the lines suggest about the characters. Discuss and record predictions about the characters and the events that students think might follow, based on these spoken lines. After the full reading, consider whether or not these predictions were correct.

Activity 1

This activity will activate prior knowledge and develop self-awareness by prompting students to consider what they already know. Students may not realise how common it is to find danger and jeopardy in stories, even those that are written for children. At this stage, students should be explicitly taught the meaning and spelling of the word 'jeopardy' and encouraged to use it accurately in their discussions and any notes they write.

Kerboodle

The following activities can be replaced by the text and activities on 3.1 *Running on the Roof of the World* worksheet.

Activity 2 Boosting your vocabulary

Widen students' vocabulary with a focus on synonyms for the words Stephen King has used which create a sense of danger. Some students could be provided with access to a dictionary or thesaurus so they can read the definition of word choices.

When they have written their own sentences, encourage students to test them on each other in pairs. They should ask their partners questions, such as: *Does each sentence work? Does it create a sense of danger?*

Activity 3 Building your knowledge

This activity requires some creative thinking and helps students to understand the physical and mental aspects of journeys. Students can be encouraged to think about the challenges from the point of view of ordinary travellers, not hardened explorers. This is a good opportunity to secure knowledge of the term 'coming-of-age' story, and discuss why this type of story is so enduring. Students could also be reminded of the work that they did on genre in Chapter 2.

Activity 4 Building your knowledge

The sequence of questions here focuses on King's characters, and how the text shows readers what they are thinking and feeling, rather than telling them. Before they answer part a, make sure that students understand the terms 'adverbs' and 'adverbials'. For part c, it may be helpful initially to present the example student answer without the given teacher comment, to allow students to form their own opinion about it and perhaps undertake some paired peer-assessment before they read what the teacher has to say. They could highlight the teacher comments in the example so they can understand what makes the example a good explanation. Students could consider times that they have used these skills before and what strategies they used.

Activity 5 Putting it all together

The table encourages students to consider each main feature of the text – setting, characters and journey – as a distinct element that contributes to the building of jeopardy. Some students may require additional guidance in finding the relevant evidence and/or constructing an explanatory comment. Such students may benefit from working in a guided group while others complete the task independently.

In part b, encourage students to not only use the table to answer the question but to regularly pause and monitor their writing by referring back to the table. After they have finished, they can use the table to check off the points they have made and review their answer.

Additional activities

With parent/carer permission, students can be shown scenes from the film *Stand By Me* that build the boys' relationships and highlight their character traits. What is understood from the film can then be compared with students' responses to the text. The key scene of the boys crossing the rail bridge is also well worth watching together and could be used as a stimulus for students' own writing about a group of characters in an episode of extreme jeopardy. Finally, hot-seat the adult versions of the four characters. In character, students can be asked to recall the day of that crossing and what they learned about themselves and each other. The answers that emerge can be used to generate empathetic writing in role.

3.2 What is a quest?

Student Book pp 122–127

Unit focus

Objectives

Students will:

- learn to identify the main features of a quest and some other story types
- explore first-person narrative and inference
- write a scene for their own quest story, using key conventions.

Unit texts

- *Medusa* Jessie Burton
- *Sir Gawain and the Green Knight* Simon Armitage **WS**

Assessment

3.2 Mini-checkpoint quiz

Key terms

- **antagonist** main opponent
- **archaic** old-fashioned, from a different historical time
- **first-person narrative** a story told by someone as if they were involved in the events themselves, using first-person pronouns, e.g. *I* and *we*
- **infer** to work something out from what is seen, said or done, even though it is not stated directly
- **internal monologue** inner speech (in someone's head)
- **nemesis** an enemy or competitor that cannot be avoided
- **simile** a comparison of one thing to another, using *as* or *like*, e.g. *He swam like a fish*
- **tone** the writer's feeling or attitude expressed towards their subject; in fiction it can also reflect a character's feelings and personality

Introduction to the unit

Unit 3.2 *What is a quest?* introduces the idea of story types using Booker's theory of seven basic plots, and asks students to explore the main features of quest stories. The unit draws on students' prior reading of Greek myths and there is scope for discussion of the heroes and villains they know. The text, an extract from *Medusa* by Jessie Burton, offers an unusual retelling of the story of Perseus, from the point of view of his nemesis. It would be helpful if students knew the traditional version of the tale beforehand. Students consider typical elements of quests, including journeys, tasks to be completed and appropriate weapons. The unit has a focus on the archaic vocabulary found in myths, and builds towards the task of writing a scene from a first-person quest narrative.

Activities

Starter activity

Students are likely to have read some Greek myths at KS2 and could be encouraged to list any mythological heroes and villains that they recall. In advance of the first lesson in the unit, students could research the story of Perseus and Medusa, and based on what they discover, create a class retelling. Pre-teaching of the terms 'antagonist' and 'protagonist' (main character) will support discussion of the way the extract reverses perspectives.

Activity 1

This activity is a starting point for discussion, either as a whole class or for students in pairs. Students can be encouraged to give examples across the seven plot types from a range of media, including gaming, film and TV, as well as from a range of cultures.

Kerboodle
The following activities can be replaced by the text and activities on 3.2 *Sir Gawain and the Green Knight* worksheet.

Activity 2 Boosting your vocabulary
Students' attention is directed to the author's word choices for each of Perseus' weapons. It will be helpful to support this work with a focus on matching reading voices to the descriptions: ask students to read the weapon descriptions aloud in different ways (for example, like a child whining, like someone whispering in awe or like an army commander shouting). Students can read the descriptions aloud in a way that matches the meaning and intent of the author's words, before they go on to create their own descriptions. Tier 2 vocabulary has been provided to help students with this, but if there is time, they can be encouraged to find their own powerful words. After re-reading the description of the sword's hilt, discuss the three questions listed, to unpick the author's word choices and their effect thoroughly.

Activity 3 Building your knowledge
The table supports students to use different parts of the text to empathise with Perseus. This is a valuable inference activity, which also draws attention to the unusual narrative perspective of this retelling. It may be useful to model the process using Medusa's words to infer Perseus' thoughts and feelings for all students, especially less fluent and mature readers.

Activity 4 Building your knowledge
Students consolidate here, building on the empathy they have developed for Perseus, to write a monologue from his perspective. Students can be encouraged to look at their answers to Activity 3 and how an author shows the internal feelings of a character. Some students may need additional support to select and apply the archaic language choices which will give their writing authenticity. It would be helpful to co-create one or two further sentences of the example work to provide an extra layer of support and demonstrate the writing choices that need to be made. This can be done with the whole class or with targeted students.

Activity 5 Putting it all together
This planning activity takes students stage-by-stage through a decision-making process, offering some prompts. Discussion of each decision will help students who struggle to form original ideas independently, and further support can be provided by viewing images of potential settings and weapons. Encourage students to create diverse and representative quester characters who break the male stereotype. Students are likely to be able to give examples of female and non-binary questers from the gaming world.

Activity 6 Putting it all together
Students now write a scene from their planned quest story, focusing on the unpacking of weapons. Drama could be used here with students acting out the withdrawal of each item and showing by their actions and reactions its weight, appearance and curiosity value. Key features for the writing are suggested but, if possible, elicit students' own ideas for the best writing, then use these co-constructed success criteria as part of self- and peer-assessment. Encourage students to write several lines about each weapon, describing them in detail, showing the narrator's response and building the sense of each item's importance. Writing 'a lot about a little' is key to success. Modelling ways to begin or example sentences that deliver the key features will support most students.

Stretch yourself
This activity allows students to consider multiple perspectives and write from the perspective of an observer rather than the character doing the action. Encourage students to consider the idea of a nemesis, as introduced earlier in the unit.

Additional activities
Students could discuss the links between self-discovery and a quest story, e.g. the obstacles that characters face in quest stories are symbols for the challenges in real life. For a home learning activity, students could be asked to write a full quest story, or to edit, improve and publish a polished draft of the 'unpacking the weapons' scene. Students can also read (or re-read) other well-known quest stories, such as *Beowulf* or *The Hobbit* or watch a film like *Finding Nemo, The Wizard of Oz* or *Jumanji: Welcome to the Jungle*, reporting back on how it qualifies as a quest.

3.3 Why start with a journey?

Student Book pp 128–133

Unit focus

Objectives

Students will:

- learn to recognise key plot conventions
- identify word choices and literary devices and comment on their effects
- analyse the presentation of a journey, using close textual reference.

Unit texts

- *Jamaica Inn* Daphne Du Maurier
- *The Secret Garden* Frances Hodgson Burnett **WS**

Assessment

3.3 Mini-checkpoint quiz

Key terms

- **cohesive device** a word or phrase that links ideas together, e.g. *at the beginning, however, although*
- **context** the words that come before and after a particular word or phrase and help to clarify its meaning
- **foreshadowing** a technique that gives a hint of something that will develop later
- **inciting incident** the event that sets up the action for the rest of the story
- **pathetic fallacy** giving emotions to something non-human in the natural world to reflect a character's feelings or situation
- **protagonist** main character

Introduction to the unit

Unit 3.3 *Why start with a journey?* builds on students' understanding of jeopardy (Unit 3.1) and examines the journey as a plot convention for launching characters and their narrative arcs. The opening of *Jamaica Inn* helps students understand why writers may choose to begin with a journey. Although the novel was published in 1936, it is set in 1816 and Du Maurier adopts the style and tone of a Victorian novel, so students will grapple with some archaic syntax and vocabulary choices. By the end of the unit, they will be able to write about this text in detail, commenting on the author's intent in the style of a literary essay.

Activities

Starter activity

Invite students to share memories of texts they have read or films they know that start with journeys. For example, *The Parent Trap* (1998) begins with two girls from different backgrounds arriving at summer camp, while Studio Ghibli's *My Neighbour Totoro* (1988) opens with a family en route to a new home. Discuss how the characters might feel on such a journey, what might be in store for them (positives and negatives), and the advantages for storytellers of starting with characters in transit, about to arrive somewhere new.

Activity 1

This activity is best done in pairs. Examples could include: four children travel to a snowy otherworld (*The Lion, the Witch and the Wardrobe*), a girl travels from India to live on the Yorkshire Moors (Mary Lennox in *The Secret Garden*), a character being called to action (Princess Leia's message to Obi Wan Kenobi in *Star Wars*), a first romantic meeting (*Romeo and Juliet*) or the arrival of a new person (Magwitch in *Great Expectations* or a terrifying little girl in *Monsters, Inc.*). For part b, students could discuss what makes them want to read a book and what keeps them reading.

Kerboodle

The following activities can be replaced by the text and activities on 3.3 *The Secret Garden* worksheet.

Activity 2 Boosting your vocabulary

To check students' understanding of familiar vocabulary being used in unfamiliar ways, this activity needs to be completed independently. If students are unable to work out how the words are being used, this will be an indication that further re-reading of the text is required. Build fluency through repeated reading, beginning with a modelled read-aloud and moving on to a performative read in pairs, in which students focus on adjusting tone and volume, as well as placing pauses and emphasis in a way that reinforces meaning and the atmosphere of the piece. Part b works as a whole-class activity and can be made more active by writing out the words on large sheets of paper and physically placing them on a line across the classroom.

Activity 3 Building your knowledge

Students need to be familiar with finding apt quotations. Discuss the example in the table with students and ask them if they think the quotation supports the statement. For the next statement, focus on selecting an appropriate and precise quotation that is short and highly illustrative of the key point. Model the thought process about how to identify the change and how to identify a supporting quotation.

Activity 4 Building your knowledge

In this activity, students learn about pathetic fallacy. Initially locating examples in the text, they then look at how the technique reveals character. To extend students' understanding, they can consider how different weather descriptions and changes (the sun coming out, a thunderstorm or a blizzard) can be used to suggest other mood or character shifts.

Activity 5 Building your knowledge

Students are asked to look at elements in the story and how these hint at what might happen to Mary. This could be done as a whole-class discussion or students can work in pairs. Encourage them to look for the clue in the text to help them with their answers.

Activity 6 Building your knowledge

Students are presented with one annotated first draft paragraph, then a second improved version. More confident students could be shown just the first paragraph and asked to suggest improvements of their own, before comparing their ideas to the remarks of the teacher. This would also work well as an activity pairing a more confident student with a less confident student, to work together to identify areas for improvement. Students could work alone to annotate a copy of the second draft paragraph showing how the improvements suggested by the teacher have been acted upon by the student.

Stretch yourself

With a focus on wider reading and making connections between texts, this activity could be set as a homework task or turned into another full lesson, if texts are provided.

Activity 7 Putting it all together

Students write formally about the *Jamaica Inn* extract. The example provided as a first draft in Activity 6 can be used as a tool to build success criteria, as it highlights how **not** to complete the task. Teacher modelling will provide support here, especially with a focus on the use of cohesive devices to connect points together. Students could also use their answers from Activities 5 and 6 as they have already identified the features, found the evidence and considered the author's intentions. Self-assessment can be enhanced by shared peer-assessment first, with two or three students' work edited and improved jointly through class discussion before individuals review their own writing.

Additional activities

Students choose a text or film that begins with a journey, and give a short presentation about it to the class, explaining how it demonstrates the plot convention of a journey as an inciting incident, and the way it reveals characterisation and sets the scene for what will happen next.

3.4 How can poetry explore journeys?

Student Book pp 134–139

Unit focus

Objectives

Students will:

- learn how texts are influenced by the contexts in which they are written
- rehearse and perform a poetry reading
- recognise poetic features and comment on their effect.

Unit texts

- 🔊 'Things We Carry on the Sea' Wang Ping
- Ⓚ 'An Escape' Ha Jin **WS**

Assessment

Ⓚ 3.4 Mini-checkpoint quiz; Chapter 3 Checkpoint 1 reading assessment; Chapter 3 Checkpoint 1 writing assessment

Key terms

- **abstract** existing as an idea but not having a physical reality
- **audience** the people or person for whom a text is written or performed
- **ellipsis** three dots (...) used to show a pause or to indicate that a word or words have been left out
- **first-person plural pronoun** *we* and *us* are ways of speaking in the first person about more than one person
- **recital** a performance
- **repetition** using the same word or phrase more than once
- **stanza** a group of lines in a poem with a line space before and after it

Introduction to the unit

Unit 3.4 *How can poetry explore journeys?* highlights the importance of context, as well as providing an opportunity for poetry performance and analysis. Students move on from exploring journeys in fiction to considering accounts of real-life refugee journeys. Sensitivity will be required as many students may be concerned about refugees whom they have seen in the news, and the class may contain students who have experienced flight or displacement. The poem in this unit was written by Wang Ping. She grew up in China during the time when the ruling Communist party was using extreme and often violent methods to impose their ideas. She left China and moved to the USA.

Activities

Starter activity

Students can research the many reasons why people throughout history have migrated – for work, for land, to escape war or persecution, or in flight from natural disaster. This research task should include checking the definitions of terms that will support informed discussion of the relevant issues, such as 'migration', 'immigration', 'economic migrant', 'asylum seeker' and 'refugee'. Ensure students appreciate the differences and similarities between voluntary migration and forced displacement, including the slave trade and human trafficking. The UN High Commissioner for Refugees website provides helpful, accurate information.

Activity 1

Sharing information as a whole class is key to exposing misconceptions that need to be addressed. Students draw on their prior knowledge as well as beliefs that might underlie particular attitudes. The prompts are designed to help students empathise with migrants. These should be used with care, especially if students have personal experience. It is important to create a climate in which students can share ideas and views, but are challenged if these are hateful or intolerant.

Kerboodle
The following activities can be replaced by the text and activities on 3.4 'An Escape' worksheet.

Activity 2
It is likely that re-reading the poem several times will help students to respond to these comprehension questions. The questions check literal understanding and also prompt thoughts about some of the poetic features, which can be used as a starting point for initial discussion about the poem. Students may benefit from noting their answers in writing to refer back to when they look more analytically at the poem later in the unit.

Activity 3
Depending on students' prior experience of recital, they may benefit from additional preparation, such as watching video of poets reciting poems and evaluating the effective aspects of performance. Students could also discuss about speaking aloud to the class in previous units. If students are going to perform to the class, consider using a group approach to avoid too much repetition. If there are students or colleagues in the school who have knowledge of the languages used in the poem (Mandarin Chinese, Spanish, Yiddish and Arabic), bring them in as expert advisors.

Activity 4 Boosting your vocabulary
This activity draws attention to the ways language changes and the influence of American culture on modern English. Students can discuss what other American terms they know. Speakers of different variations of English could give examples of similarities and differences. Students' own languages, dialects and accents can also be celebrated here.

Activity 5 Building your knowledge
As a whole class, read the information about the poem. At this point, students will benefit from having a copy of the poem in front of them that they can annotate or annotate the poem on a screen. Support students to identify the features of the poem that are explained, and to highlight illustrative quotations. It may be necessary to model this, building on the example provided, to show students how to incorporate key terms into their explanations of effect. When students are ready, whole-class work can segue into pair or individual work.

Activity 6 Putting it all together
Building on the analytical writing they did about *Jamaica Inn* in Unit 3.3, students now write in a similar formal way about the poem. Encourage students to use their answers from Activity 5 to support them with this activity. When students think they have finished, they should check their work. For example, they can:

- swap writing with another student and share information, knowledge or ideas that would improve their work
- read aloud the whole poem and their paragraphs about it, before making corrections to syntax and expression to make sure points are clear.

Additional activities
Students could write their own 'we carry' poems. They could draw on the journey of their life as inspiration or adopt the persona of a grandparent or elderly neighbour, or create someone imaginary. To help them to make a start, ask students to make a list of the real, physical things that might be carried through life, such as schoolbags, backpacks, phones or scars from childhood accidents. Make another list of more abstract things that are carried, such as the names of lost pets, memories of special people or places, hopes and ambitions for the future. Students can be encouraged to borrow words and phrases from Wang Ping's poem and to use it as a structural prop for their own writing. The poems they write may vary in tone and style – perhaps poignant, contemplative, factual, hopeful or celebratory.

3.5 What is travel writing?

Student Book pp 140–145

Unit focus

Objectives

Students will:

- learn about the key conventions of travel writing
- identify the effects of grammatical features in travel writing
- write about a journey around their neighbourhood.

Unit texts

- Blog post on alastairhumphreys.com Alastair Humphreys
- A letter from Lady Montagu **WS**

Assessment

3.5 Mini-checkpoint quiz

Key terms

- **adjective** and **adjectival phrase** a word or phrase that describes a person or thing
- **autobiographical** based on the writer's life
- **contrast** difference between two or more things; also, to compare to show a difference
- **minor sentence** sometimes known as a sentence fragment, a sentence without a main verb or subject
- **non-fiction** real events or factual information
- **noun phrase** a noun plus information before and/or after the noun
- **prepositional phrase** a phrase that begins with a preposition (e.g. *between, near, by, beyond*) and tells the reader about location and place
- **travel writing** writing produced during or after a journey, describing it in order to inform and/ or entertain readers
- **verb** a word or group of words that express an action, event or state, e.g. the boy *eats*, tigers *prowl*, the building *exists*

Introduction to the unit

Unit 3.5 *What is travel writing?* introduces students to the history and conventions of travel writing via a non-fiction text. From the 17th and 18th centuries, wealthy young men went on an educational rite-of-passage trip around Europe called The Grand Tour, studying history and languages, exploring the arts and mountaineering. Until relatively recently, it was rare for women to travel independently, although some did. For example, Austrian Ida Laura Pfeiffer (1797–1858) travelled over 32,000 kilometres on land and 240,000 kilometres by sea during her lifetime. Some students will know of Jamaican nurse Mary Seacole from their history work in KS2, but may not be aware of her book *Wonderful Adventures of Mary Seacole in Many Lands* (1857). It is important that students approach this unit feeling that travel writing is not only for those with the time and resources to travel far afield on exotic adventures. Nowadays, a travel writer may be someone exploring their local neighbourhood and posting about it on a blog or vlog.

Activities

Starter activity

Encourage students to investigate a selection of maps, travel brochures, tourism websites and travel books. Discuss places, near and far, that students would like to visit and why. Consider the personal, and global, pros and cons of travel. For example, the thrill of seeing new sights, as well as the expense and the environmental cost of travel. Pairs of students could list six to eight reasons to travel (such as 'to learn about different cultures' or 'to get away from home') for another pair to rank in order of agreement.

Activity 1

Students should consider these statements before they read the extract from Alastair Humphreys' blog. By the end of the unit, they should be able to write their own list of factual statements about travel writing.

Kerboodle

The following activities can be replaced by the text and activities on 3.5 Lady Montagu's letter worksheet.

Activity 2 Boosting your vocabulary

Students' inference skills are developed in this multiple-choice activity – they will need to read the text carefully and not depend solely on their prior understanding of the target vocabulary. When they use the words in their own sentences, take the opportunity to discuss use of 'landscaped' and 'demolished' as verbs and adjectives.

Activity 3 Building your knowledge

Alastair Humphreys is a National Geographic Adventurer of the Year and has been taking on challenging journeys since he was a child. As a teenager, he cycled off-road across England. Later, he cycled around the world, rowed across the Atlantic and crossed Iceland by foot. His writing is published on his blog and in numerous books. In this text he describes a very local trip, a 'microadventure' which his readers can emulate. Activity 3 draws students' attention to the key features of the text, thus introducing them to the conventions of travel writing. The activity can be completed as a whole class with students racing each other to locate each feature, or at a slower pace in pairs.

Activity 4 Building your knowledge

Students prepare for the final task in the unit by focusing on grammatical features of travel writing. They can work independently or in groups, compiling larger versions of the table, for example on flipchart paper. It can be displayed for later use as a checklist of success criteria when students are working on their own writing.

Activity 5 Putting it all together

As steps 1 and 2 of this activity take place outside, relevant permissions and trip policies need to be referenced. It could also be set as a homework activity. Use maps of the local area to plan students' journeys, identifying key buildings or sites to notice as they travel. Encourage them to notice the minutiae of their journey and at each stage include small, specific details, like the exact colour of a wall, the fabric of a passer-by's clothes or the precise sound of a vehicle going past. If they cannot go on an actual journey, students could use Google Maps and Street View to plot a virtual one.

An example paragraph plan is offered, but some students may prefer to plan their writing in different ways, for example by annotating a map of their route, using a flow chart structured around key places on their journey or taking photos and making notes on a mobile device as they go.

Activity 6 Putting it all together

As a whole class, decide on some success criteria about what a successful first draft would look like; use the features that have already been discussed. Stop students mid-way through their draft to monitor what they are writing and to refer back to the list of structural and grammatical features and the success criteria. When they have finished their draft, ask them to review the success criteria independently or with a partner and see if they can improve their writing.

Additional activities

Students' edited and polished writing can be collected and published, with copies placed in the school and local libraries, or sold to raise school funds. Alternatively, publish a selection on the school website. Add to this over time, with travel writing pieces about students' holiday experiences, days out and school trips. School alumni can also be encouraged to contribute.

3.6 Why travel sustainably?

Student Book pp 146–151

Unit focus

Objectives

Students will:

- learn about features of persuasive texts
- explore the effects of persuasive techniques on the reader
- write and present a speech confidently in front of an audience.

Unit texts

- 🔈 'Electric road trip through Switzerland', 'Easy train to Sweden', 'Wildlife safari, Spain' in '20 of the Best Sustainable Holidays in Europe for 2020' Gemma Bowes
- Ⓚ '7 steps to being a mindful traveller' Soraya Abdel-Hadi **WS**

Assessment

Ⓚ 3.6 Mini-checkpoint quiz

Key terms

- **alliteration** using the same letter or sound at the beginning of several words for special effect
- **colloquial language** informal words or phrases that are suitable for ordinary conversation, rather than formal speech or writing
- **direct address** addressing the reader as *you*
- **emotive language** word choices that create a strong emotional reaction in the reader
- **evidence and statistics** data and facts
- **persuasive** making you want to do or believe something
- **scanning** reading quickly to find something specific
- **technical information** specialised words or phrases

Introduction to the unit

Unit 3.6 *Why travel sustainably?* focuses on persuasive writing, in the context of sustainable travel and tourism. Students recap and extend their understanding of techniques used to promote a perspective and influence readers. Speech writing and presentation activities give an important opportunity to enhance oracy skills. Encourage students to understand the impacts of their own travel and how these can be minimised or offset. Exploit links with Geography curriculum coverage of travel and tourism impacts.

Activities

Starter activity

Set up groups of three and have two students take turns to verbally persuade each other to do something (such as watch a film in a new genre, eat something unfamiliar or donate time to a cause), while the third student observes and makes notes on the strategies used. Compile a class list of these persuasive approaches, ready to compare with the persuasive techniques used in the extract they are going on to read.

Activity 1

Discuss as a whole class students' answers to parts a–c. For part d ask students to recall any persuasive writing undertaken at primary school, and collect examples of the persuasive writing that surrounds them, from advertising hoardings to online adverts and charity appeals. Display examples in the classroom, highlighting the persuasive techniques so that students have visual access to examples of the techniques they will need to use in their speeches.

Kerboodle

The following activities can be replaced by the text and activities on 3.6 '7 steps to being a mindful traveller' worksheet.

Activity 2

The article can be read in a number of ways – as a whole class, in pairs and then individually. Students need to learn the skills of skimming and scanning a text to find evidence before they start the task. Students can practise reading the text in different voices too – downbeat and monotonous, cheerful and lively. This will help students to become familiar with vocabulary, structure and authorial stance. The true/false activity should be completed individually so that the standard of comprehension can be addressed accurately.

Activity 3 Boosting your vocabulary

For part a, list students' suggestions so that they can compare with the word 'devour'. Part b takes an etymological approach to deepen students' understanding of the word 'sustainable' and then consider its root. Enhance word study by regularly using this type of vocabulary exploration to help students build stronger knowledge of links between words with common roots.

Activity 4 Building your knowledge

Students need to re-read the article extracts to find examples of the listed techniques. They will then match the definition and effect to the techniques located. Some students will require support with this task and will benefit from working in a collaborative group or under close teacher guidance. More confident readers who would benefit from additional challenge could be provided with another text containing similar features (such as an extract from an eco-travel brochure), so that they can apply learning more independently.

Activity 5 Building your knowledge

Students will benefit from working in pairs or small groups to research sustainable travel. They also might benefit from sourcing other reference material or access to the Internet. For parts b and c, students begin to plan their own eco-friendly holiday and rehearse persuasive techniques at sentence level. These can be tested verbally on a partner and refined, as well as being displayed in the classroom as inspiration and/or support for all.

Stretch yourself

Make sure students refer to the extracts and the techniques and encourage them to work in pairs.

Activity 6 Putting it all together

This planning activity is designed to help students prepare, step-by-step, for their verbal presentation. Give students options for planning, such as:

- mind maps: tell students to put the holiday title in the middle of the page and add thought-bubbles for each persuasive technique
- box-plan: tell students to fold a piece of A3 paper into eight rectangles and identify eight different selling points. They can make a note on each rectangle.

Many students may not have spoken formally from notes in front of an audience before, so consider creating class rules and expectations to ensure a minimum standard, including around the use of notes and slides. Speeches are likely to be of higher quality if displayed text is kept to a minimum and there is instead an emphasis on visual engagement through props and images.

Activity 7 Putting it all together

Students will need time either during or outside lessons to prepare for delivering their speeches. As far as possible, allow every student to have their turn in front of the whole class, but if this would be too daunting for some or take too long, students could deliver their speeches in small groups or recruit others to form a supportive audience.

Additional activities

Complement this unit by arranging a speaker from the travel and tourism industry, a lecturer on a local travel and tourism course or an eco-travel activist. Before they come, help students to prepare questions. After the visit, students could write about what they learned for the school newsletter or website. This will support the school in meeting the Gatsby careers education benchmarks.

3.7 Why take a risk?

Student Book pp 152–157

Unit focus

Objectives

Students will:

- learn to recognise the effect of a writer's choice of techniques in a piece of travel writing
- explore how the structure of a piece of travel writing creates excitement
- write an article about a travel adventure.

Unit texts

- 'Bungee at Victoria Falls: The Day the Void Came for Me' Deborah O'Donoghue
- 'Bungee at Victoria Falls: The Day the Void Came for Me' Part 2 Deborah O'Donoghue **WS**

Assessment

3.7 Mini-checkpoint quiz

Introduction to the unit

Unit 3.7 *Why take a risk?* takes students on an exciting journey to witness a daring travel adventure. They will read a tense description of bungee-jumping, imagine meeting the writer and finally write their own piece recounting the build-up to a risk-laden travel experience of their choice. Some students with narrower experience of the world will need additional support to be creative. Also be aware of the potential for anxiety for some students, especially those who have experienced loss related to dangerous sports or who have suffered other trauma.

Activities

Starter activity

Widen discussion and ask students to reflect on how they feel about risk-taking in general, and extreme sports in particular. Some students may already be expert in activities that others would avoid because of the physical risk – skateboarding, martial arts, mountain-biking, sea-swimming, climbing. These are all permissible and young people are often encouraged to pursue them, while other risky activities that sometimes present temptation for young people are ill-advised and even illegal (smoking, shoplifting). Relevant questions to pose include: *Does the thrill always justify the danger? Are human beings programmed to take risks? What do we learn from pushing ourselves beyond our limits?* A formal debate on one of these topics would introduce students to many issues explored implicitly in this unit.

Activity 1

Show students images or video of the activities and discuss any prior knowledge about what the adventures involve. This activity can be managed in pairs or constructed as a whole-class interactive experience, with images of each activity displayed around the room and students noting their reactions on sticky notes posted on each image. Alternatively, create a line across the classroom labelled at each end with most exciting to least exciting, and give students images of each activity to place on the line in the right position to show their attitude to it.

Kerboodle

The following activities can be replaced by the text and activities on 3.7 'Bungee at Victoria Falls' worksheet.

Activity 2 Boosting your vocabulary

This activity first aims to consolidate understanding of some of the tier 2 vocabulary in the text that may be less familiar to students. Part b begins to engage students with the writer's feelings at different stages of the adventure.

Stretch yourself

Students could be encouraged to identify the words in the extract and then discuss with a partner how they create a sense of excitement before they write their own paragraph.

Activity 3 Building your knowledge

This activity would be a good small group or paired activity. The extract could be displayed on a screen or students could be given copies of the extract. For part a, the first match could be modelled, making sure that the thought process is explicit, before students match the other summaries. For part b, students can annotate their copies of the extract to identify the words and phrases that help to show the excitement building.

Activity 4 Building your knowledge

Ensure students read the information about the techniques used in the extract. Some students will require support with this task and will benefit from working in a collaborative group or being more closely guided. Re-reading the text will also help. More confident readers should be encouraged to work independently. Provide a copy of the text for highlighting as an alternative to the table.

Activity 5 Building your knowledge

Enable complete student ownership of the writing task by encouraging them to select their own travel adventure. Some research time might be necessary to facilitate this. Students could use a mind map or a table in order to plan. These will help them group their information into paragraphs.

Activity 6 Putting it all together

This final writing activity and reflection will require students to assimilate factual research and their own ideas into an imaginative recount, and is a challenging task. Students could watch video of extreme sports in different parts of the world (try searching online for 'Spanish rooftop cycling' or 'Zambezi river rafting'). Provide support through teacher modelling, collaborative writing and structured drafting. For example, stop-target students after each paragraph to get them to self-assess that they are meeting the success criteria. The reflection on writing can be undertaken verbally, as a written exercise, via student conferencing in groups, in guided feedback sessions or as a whole-class discussion.

Stretch yourself

Students could annotate their own writing, identifying the words before they write their paragraph.

Additional activities

Students could watch more video of extreme sports in different parts of the world and write about these adventures from the point of view of the participant. Alternatively, students could write discursively about risk: *Should we ban all dangerous activities?* If possible, organise a trip to a local physical activity centre, such as a climbing wall, velodrome, trampoline park, tree-top trail or indoor ski-run. Have students write diary entries the night before and on the day of the visit, reflecting on their feelings about the level of risk and what they learn about themselves.

3.8 Can journeys tell stories?

Student Book pp 158–163

Unit focus

Objectives

Students will:

- learn about the conventions of autobiographical writing
- learn how to structure an analytical response
- write about a literary text using a formal, analytical style.

Unit texts

- *Brown Girl Dreaming* Jacqueline Woodson
- *Coming to England* Floella Benjamin **WS**

Assessment

3.8 Mini-checkpoint quiz; Chapter 3 Checkpoint 2 speaking and listening assessment; Chapter 3 Checkpoint 2 writing assessment

Key terms

- **chronological** arranged in the order in which things happened
- **embedded quotation** when a word or phrase from the text is used in a sentence about the text
- **metaphor** a comparison that says one thing *is* something else, e.g. *Amy was a rock*

Introduction to the unit

Unit 3.8 *Can journeys tell stories?* shows students the connections between autobiography and travel writing, highlighting the many features they have in common. Context is significant in this unit. Allow students to share their knowledge about civil rights campaigns of the distant and recent past. The text extract includes a dated and offensive term, and it's important to ensure students are aware of the appropriate language to use when talking about race issues.

Activities

Starter activity

Either as pre-learning at home or as a class, students should browse Jacqueline Woodson's website. Invite them to read about the books she has written and watch her TED Talk about her childhood reading and how it influenced her. Encourage students to try reading some of her novels, such as:

- *Hush* – two sisters have to reinvent themselves in a witness protection programme
- *Before the Ever After* – football-star dad suffers severe head injuries and suddenly he seems like a different person
- *Last Summer with Maizon* – the story of a Black girl at an all-white boarding school.

Activity 1

Students could be asked to discuss the word 'autobiography'. Link to work on prefixes to find that 'auto' means 'self', and then etymology to find that 'graph' is from the Ancient Greek word *graphos*, meaning 'to write'. Students can be asked what they know about autobiography from their learning at KS2 and any examples that they have read and be asked whether they enjoyed reading them, giving reasons for why or why not.

Kerboodle
The following activities can be replaced by the text and activities on 3.8 *Coming to England* worksheet.

Activity 2 Boosting your vocabulary
Students will need to read the text carefully to locate the target words. Once they have written their own definitions, agree on those that are clearest. Compare student definitions with dictionary definitions and extend the task, if desired, by having students write their own passage that uses each of the target words correctly.

Activity 3 Building your knowledge
For part a, make sure that students have understood the features of autobiography and then some students will need support in finding the examples in the text. It might be helpful if they work in pairs or small groups. For part b, students could discuss in small groups and then feed back to the whole class.

Activity 4 Building your knowledge
Students could create a table to present their evidence. Model finding evidence for one of the notes about features. Explicitly, talk through what isn't evidence and explain why, as well as explaining what is evidence.

Stretch yourself
Students should be encouraged to look back at Units 3.1 and 3.3 to link the physical and inner journeys and the meaning of the word 'autobiography'.

Activity 5 Building your knowledge
Make sure that the text has been fully discussed before students prepare to write about it. The following types of questions will help students to focus on key aspects:

- *Why does the writer use different voices to tell her story?*
- *What feelings do the adults in the text reveal?*
- *What aspects of the journey are challenging?*
- *How do we know the children are loved and well cared-for?*

Activity 6 Putting it all together
Building on the practice they have had earlier in this chapter, students are expected to write at length in a formal way, adopting an analytical approach. Guidance for paragraph planning is provided, but by this stage, students have used a number of different planning methods and should be given the opportunity to choose what works for them.

Additional activities
Invite students to read the whole of Jacqueline Woodson's verse autobiography *Brown Girl Dreaming* and ask them to write to the author, explaining their reactions to it and what they have learned. Broaden students' reading by providing extracts from *I Know Why the Caged Bird Sings* by Maya Angelou and Thanhha Lai's *Inside Out & Back Again*, a novel based on the author's childhood experiences as a refugee.

Quest key terms glossary

abstract existing as an idea but not having a physical reality

abstract noun a noun that refers to an idea, quality or emotion, rather than a solid object, e.g. *happiness, truth, freedom*

adjectival phrase a phrase that describe a person or thing

adjective a word that describes a noun

adverb a word that you use with a verb, adjective or other adverb that tells you how, when or where something happened

adverbial a word or phrase that explains how, where, or when something happened, or shows how ideas relate to one another

alliteration using the same letter or sound at the beginning of several words for special effect

anecdote a short or entertaining story about real people or events

antagonist main opponent

antonym a word that has the opposite meaning of a particular word

archaic old-fashioned, from a different historical time

audience the people or person for whom a text is written or performed

autobiographical based on the writer's life

bilingual able to speak two languages

byline a line at the beginning or end of a newspaper or magazine article that gives the writer's name

character a person in a drama or story

characterisation the methods an author uses to create a character, e.g. describing how they look, the use of dialogue or showing how they treat others

chronological arranged in the order in which things happened

cliffhanger an exciting event at the end of a chapter, leaving the reader anxious and eager to know what happens next

climax when the action is at its most exciting or interesting

code-switching moving between different levels of formality in language, e.g. between Standard English and non-standard English

cohesive device a word or phrase that links ideas together, e.g. *at the beginning, however, although*

colloquial language informal words or phrases that are suitable for ordinary conversation, rather than formal speech or writing

coming-of-age story a story in which characters experience things that teach them about adulthood

commentary a written explanation or discussion

compare judge how two or more things are similar and different

compound word a word that is made up of two or more other words. Some compound words have hyphens, but not all, e.g. *ear-splitting, suitcase, hedgehog*

conflict a struggle or disagreement between people

conjunction a linking word, e.g. *if, and, but*

connective a general term for a word or phrase that helps link information

connotation an idea or feeling linked to a word, as well as its main meaning

context the time, place and influences on a text from when it was written, and from when it is read, which shape our understanding of the text; also, the words that come before and after a particular word or phrase and help to clarify its meaning

contrast difference between two or more things; also, to compare to show a difference

convention a typical feature you find in a particular genre

debate to have a formal discussion in which opposite views on a subject are heard fairly

dialect a form of a language linked to a specific region, e.g. Geordie in Newcastle upon Tyne

dialogue words spoken by characters

direct address addressing the reader as *you*

drama a play written for performance on stage or to be listened to

editorial a newspaper article expressing a writer's opinion

ellipsis three dots (...) used to show a pause or to indicate that a word or words have been left out

embedded quotation when a word or phrase from the text is used in a sentence about the text

emotive language word choices that create a strong emotional reaction in the reader

empathy the ability to understand and share in someone else's feelings

evidence and statistics data and facts

explicit stating something openly and exactly

fantasy an imaginary story that is not based on reality

fiction a narrative that is imaginary or invented

figurative language words or phrases with a meaning that is different from the literal meaning

first-person narrative a story told by someone as if they were involved in the events themselves, using first-person pronouns, e.g. *I* and *we*

first-person plural pronoun *we* and *us* are ways of speaking in the first person about more than one person

fluency speaking with a smooth flow, without hesitating

foreshadowing a technique that gives a hint of something that will develop later

form the organisation of writing in a particular way, e.g. a letter or a poem

genre a type of story, e.g. *horror, romance, adventure, science fiction*

gesture using your hands to indicate meaning, e.g. to help emphasise certain points

headline the title of a news article printed in large letters

hyperbole exaggeration

imperative verb a verb that commands or instructs the reader

implicit not stated directly, but suggested or hinted at

inciting incident the event that sets up the action for the rest of the story

infer to work something out from what is seen, said or done, even though it is not stated directly

internal monologue inner speech (in someone's head)
juvenile linked to young people
juxtaposition putting words, ideas or images together, especially to show a contrast or relationship between them
literary terminology current and precise words for techniques writers use
metaphor a comparison that says one thing *is* something else, e.g. *Amy was a rock*
minor sentence sometimes known as a sentence fragment, a sentence without a main verb or subject
modal verb a verb that works with another verb to show that something needs to happen or might possibly happen, e.g. *must, shall, will, should, would, can, could, may,* and *might*
monologue a speech by one character
mythical from a myth, a traditional story that often includes supernatural beings
narrative a story or account of connected events
narrative voice the perspective (viewpoint) from which a story is told, and the style in which it is told
narrator a person who tells a story, especially in a book, play or film
nemesis an enemy or competitor that cannot be avoided
non-fiction real events or factual information
non-narrative information that is not part of a sequence of events
non-standard English an informal version of English, often used with family and friends, including slang and regional variations
noun phrase a noun plus information before and/or after the noun
objective not influenced by personal feeling or opinion
onomatopoeia words that imitate or suggest what they stand for, e.g. *cuckoo, sizzle*
pace the speed at which someone moves or something happens
pathetic fallacy giving emotions to something non-human in the natural world to reflect a character's feelings or situation
persuasive making you want to do or believe something
poetry a piece of writing often arranged in short lines and stanzas, following a pattern of sounds, and expressing feelings and ideas with great imagination
prefix a word or group of letters placed in front of another word to add to or change its meaning
prepositional phrase a phrase that begins with a preposition (e.g. *between, near, by, beyond*) and tells the reader about location and place
pronoun a word used instead of a noun or noun phrase, e.g. *he, it, they*
prose written language in its ordinary form, rather than poetry or drama
protagonist main character
pun a play on words to help entertain the reader
purpose the reason that a text is written
quotation a word or phrase from a text
recital a performance
register the manner of speaking or writing, which can range between formal and informal
repetition using the same word or phrase more than once
rhetorical question a question asked for dramatic effect and not intended to get an answer
rhyme using the same sound to end words, particularly at the ends of lines
rhythm the pattern of beats in a line of music or poetry
scanning reading quickly to find something specific
sensationalist presented in a deliberate way to stir up excitement and interest
setting where the action takes place
simile a comparison of one thing to another, using *as* or *like*, e.g. *He swam like a fish*
stage direction an instruction to an actor about movement or expression, or a description of a sound effect
Standard English a widely recognised formal version of English, not linked to any region, but used in schools, exams, official publications and in public announcements
standfirst a sentence or two beneath a headline, but before the main body of an article, which introduces what follows
stanza a group of lines in a poem with a line space before and after it
structural feature a feature used by a writer to give a text its overall shape
subject the person or thing that does the verb, e.g. *the boy* eats, *tigers* prowl, *the building* exists
subjective influenced by personal feeling or opinion
suffix a word or group of letters placed at the end of another word or root to add to or change its meaning
suspense a feeling of anxious uncertainty while waiting for something to happen or become known
symbol something specific that represents a more general quality or situation
synonym a word or phrase that means the same, or almost the same, as another word or phrase
synthesise to combine separate parts into something new
technical information specialised words or phrases
tension being on edge with nerves stretched tight
text any form of written material
third-person narrative a story told by someone who was not involved in the events themselves, using third-person pronouns, e.g. *he, she, they*
tone the writer's feeling or attitude expressed towards their subject; in fiction it can also reflect a character's feelings and personality
transcript a written record of spoken words
travel writing writing produced during or after a journey, describing it in order to inform and/or entertain readers
tricolon a pattern of three words or phrases grouped together to be memorable and have impact
unreliable narrator a narrator who may or may not prove to be trustworthy, either intentionally or otherwise
verb a word or group of words that express an action, event or state, e.g. the boy *eats*, tigers *prowl*, the building *exists*

OXFORD
UNIVERSITY PRESS

Great Clarendon Street, Oxford, OX2 6DP, United Kingdom

Oxford University Press is a department of the University of Oxford. It furthers the University's objective of excellence in research, scholarship, and education by publishing worldwide. Oxford is a registered trade mark of Oxford University Press in the UK and in certain other countries.

Authors: Helen Backhouse, Jane Branson and Jenny Roberts

First published in 2023

British Library Cataloguing in Publication Data
Data available

978-1-38-2033299

978-1-38-2033305

10 9 8 7 6 5 4 3 2 1

Paper used in the production of this book is a natural, recyclable product made from wood grown in sustainable forests.

The manufacturing process conforms to the environmental regulations of the country of origin.

Printed in Great Britain by CPI Group (UK) Ltd., Croydon CR0 4YY

Acknowledgements
The publisher and authors would like to thank the following for permission to use copyright material:

Artwork by Michael Driver.

Every effort has been made to contact copyright holders of material reproduced in this book. Any omissions will be rectified in subsequent printings if notice is given to the publisher.